WITNESS AMONG FRIENDS

Cliff Christians

A joint publication by

Office of Education and Faith Development
and
Office of Evangelism and Church Development
Reformed Church in America

Evangelism Department, Board of Home Missions
and
Education Department, CRC Publications
Christian Reformed Church in North America

Acknowledgments

The publishers are grateful to Dr. Cliff Christians for writing this book. Dr. Christians is Research Professor of Communications and Director of the Institute of Communications Research at the University of Illinois.

We also thank Rev. Tim Brown, Minister of Worship at Christ Memorial Reformed Church, Holland, Michigan, for pilot-teaching *Witness Among Friends* and for writing a leader's guide to accompany this book.

Copyright © 1989, CRC Publications, 2850 Kalamazoo Avenue SE, Grand Rapids, Michigan 49560

5 4 3 2 1

Library of Congress Cataloging-in-Publication Data

Christians, Clifford G.
    Witness among friends/Cliff Christians.
        p.   cm.
    Bibliography: p.
    1. Witness bearing (Christianity) 2. Friendship—Religious aspects—Christianity. I. Title.
BV4520.C55   1989
248'.5—dc19   89-818
                                                              CIP

ISBN 0-930265-61-0

CONTENTS

PREFACE

This book—and the course for which it serves as text—is sponsored by four agencies in two churches. The evangelism and church education offices in both the Reformed Church in America and the Christian Reformed Church in North America have joined in this effort.

The purpose of this project is to help ordinary church members—the 90 percent (or more) not gifted in evangelism—discover how they can witness through friendship relationships to their faith in Jesus Christ. Evangelism and church education meet naturally in this book on witnessing.

The two sponsoring churches also join naturally because they spring from related roots, hold common traditions, and share one purpose—to equip church members to reach out with the message of God's grace in Christ to those outside the church.

This book is not intended merely to increase your understanding of witnessing or to promote a new method for doing evangelism. It is meant to aid you—and others with you, if you study this as a class—in the process of transforming ordinary human relationships into living channels for witness to the love of God.

In Cliff Christians we found an ideal author for this text. He combines an expert knowledge of communication, teaching ability, and a deep concern for the gospel ministry of Christ's church. A leader's guide by Tim Brown emerges out of his congregation's actual experience with the materials of this text.

We hope and pray that this book may aid many of you to "speak the truth in love" and so witness to the goodness of God in Jesus Christ.

Robert L. Bast
Minister for Evangelism and Church
Development
Reformed Church in America

Kenneth R. Bradsell
Minister for Education and Faith Development
Reformed Church in America

Dirk J. Hart
Director of Evangelism
Board of Home Missions
Christian Reformed Church in North America

Harvey A. Smit
Editor in Chief, Education Department
CRC Publications
Christian Reformed Church in North America

INTRODUCTION

We have discussed evangelism over enough coffee to float a battleship. From the boardrooms of our denominational offices to our living rooms, we concoct strategies and lament our failure to keep pace with an exploding world population.

Let's try once more.

A major report on witnessing concluded some years ago, in a glib but illuminating way: "Biblical evangelism is above all else evangelism that is done." During the next few weeks we'll get underway—we'll start to "do." We need no fancy equipment. No million-dollar budgets. No snake-oil tactics and clever tongues. We won't even ask you to form a committee this time.

Our preoccupation is friendship. Friends are the beginning and the end of our time together. "Life is fortified by friendships," says Sydney Smith. We know this is true because we have heard that precious word from the Master himself: "You are my friends" (John 15:12–17). Friendship is one of God's greatest gifts to us.

> *Friendship is the springboard to every other love. Friendships spill over onto the other important relationships of life. People with no friends usually have a diminished capacity for sustaining any kind of love . . . . Those who learn how to love their friends tend to make long and fulfilling marriages, get along well with the people at work, and enjoy their children.*
>
> The Friendship Factor by Alan Loy McGinnis, p. 9

Remember the number 94 and you will have caught the underlying principle of these chapters. What I'm referring to is Flavil Yeakley's study of 720 newly evangelized people who were asked in which category the person who had evangelized them fell: friend, salesperson, or teacher.

> *The results provided some startling conclusions: The people who saw the church member as a "friend" were almost all new Christians and active in their churches (94 percent). On the other hand, those people who saw the church member as a "salesperson" often made an initial decision but soon dropped out in large numbers (71 percent) . . . . Those who saw the church member as a "teacher" generally tended not to respond at all (84 percent said "no thanks").*
>
> Evangelism as a Lifestyle by Jim Petersen, pp. 124–25

Ninty-four percent among friends! Hucksters may manipulate a decision, but only 29 percent of their "converts" stay. And our success rate is down to 16 percent when we "peddle the Word of God" (2 Cor. 2:17) as boring instructors. Outreach by friendship. Life-style witness. Good-news people. Witness with a loving center. Whatever label you choose, the idea is to provide natural bridges for witness. Healthy friendships are the frontline weapon, daily relationships the ultimate evangelistic tool.

We typically equate evangelism with leading people to conversion. Some of you may have tried to call someone to faith but then withdrew, humiliated and minus results. *Witness Among Friends* offers a different approach. Christians are the salt of the earth, and if we can recover our ability to befriend non-Christians, our lives as witnesses will prosper. As we cultivate human relationships in everyday living, we will discover happy opportunities to give God glory with our words. In biblical terms every Christian is a witness. If witnessing means pointing to God's activity in our lives and the world, then the church is a witnessing people. Witness-bearing is the natural result of the Holy Spirit's enabling. In *Pentecost and Missions* Harry Boer has demonstrated that the phenomenal expansion of the early church arose not from conscious obedience to the command of Christ but from spontaneous response to the Spirit's descent.

The characteristic New Testament word is not *preaching* but *marturia* (witness). Announcing the good news? Certainly. Seizing every opportunity? Absolutely. Life witness leads to verbal witness. Because questions are best asked and answered in relationships, friendships open doors. Direct calls to conversion when the Holy Spirit prepares the way? Indeed. But words always wafted along on the wings of friendship.

The goal of *Witness Among Friends* is to sharpen skills for everyday witness. To capture the realism of ongoing movement, storytelling is part of every chapter. Our goal here is not detachment and cool analysis but rather learning on our feet to establish rapport as situations unfold. Ninety-four percent.

Afraid to teach and unwilling to manipulate? Welcome to this opportunity to sharpen your skills in friend-making.

—Cliff Christians

NE

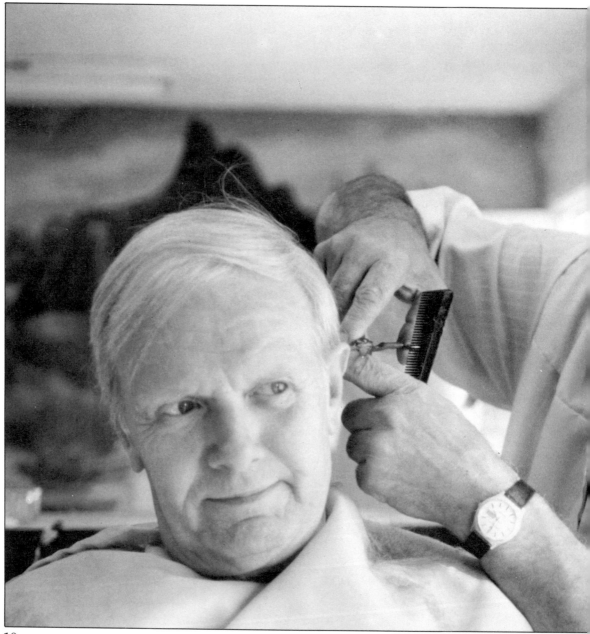

PEOPLE EYES

Fruitful witnessing begins with people eyes— eyes trained to see other people as God sees them. To God humans are priceless, made in God's image, members of the human family. God knows each of our names, feelings, rights, problems.

Often we don't have people eyes. We are content to keep our contacts with others superficial—to see other people not as individuals but as bodies that flirt across our paths.

Remember the dramatic New Testament story of the blind man who needed a second touch (Mark 8:22–26)? When Jesus first touched him, the man could see people, but not clearly. They looked like "trees walking." It took a second touch to completely restore the man's vision—to help him really see the people around him.

Pray that a similar transformation will occur in our lives. Pray that the vague personages bouncing around us will come into sharp focus, that on the second touch we will see them as potential members of the family of God.

Sometimes Satan tricks us into believing that God upholds the universe and eternity but has little to do with everyday situations. We start to forget that our location and work and gifts and circumstances are controlled by God's providence. Let's ask God to focus our eyes. Let's ask him to use these materials to help us see people not as ornamental bushes along the sidewalk or as conversion scalps on our hunting belt, but as divinely appointed friends.

Bible Study: 1 Corinthians 9:19–23

▶1. To close the communications gap with the people he was trying to reach, Paul adapted his life-style readily, taking seriously the values and customs of the unevangelized. Does this bother you, even subtly? If so, how? Why?

▶2. Paul instructs us not to conform to the world (Rom. 12:1–2) and to keep ourselves unspotted. In another famous passage (1 Cor. 5:9–11) he warns Corinthian Christians not to associate with immoral persons *within* the church.

If we are to be adept in establishing contacts, in what areas, if any, should we keep a safe distance?

▶3. Are we really to use "all possible means" to "save some"? Aren't there some techniques that defy the integrity of the gospel?

▶4. According to an old proverb, God gave us things to use but people to enjoy. How do we avoid manipulating, or using, people as we witness? Consider the two examples below as you answer this question.

a. The Moonies disguise their intentions from the beginning, using friendship as a trap to catch converts. None of us appreciates such trickery. We don't like to be caught by religious con-artists, taken by door-to-door salesmen, or subtly manipulated by family members and friends. How does having people eyes for making contacts differ from manipulating people?

Though I am free and belong to no man, I make myself a slave to everyone, to win as many as possible. To the Jews I became like a Jew, to win the Jews. To those under the law I became like one under the law (though I myself am not under the law), so as to win those under the law. To those not having the law I became like one not having the law . . . so as to win those not having the law. To the weak I became weak, to win the weak. I have become all things to all men so that by all possible means I might save some. I do all this for the sake of the gospel, that I may share in its blessings.

1 Corinthians 9:19–23

b. In *The Brothers Karamazov*, Dostoevsky pictures Ivan, the intellectual, debating intensely with his younger brother Alyosha:

> *"Imagine that you are creating a fabric of human destiny with the object of making men happy in the end, giving them peace and rest at last, but that it was essential and inevitable to torture to death only one tiny creature . . . and to found that ediface on its unavenged tears. Would you consent to be the architect on those conditions? Tell me, and tell the truth."*
>
> *"No, I wouldn't consent,"* says Alyosha softly.

Alyosha would not attack or destroy another person even if that one death resulted in peace on earth. Do you share his absolute ban on manipulation for any reason? Are you so eager to avoid even the appearance of manipulation that you have serious doubts about all forms of evangelism, including friendship witness? Explain.

Because of exposure to unhealthy evangelism models, the evangelism enterprise has been hurt. Often it is the methodology of some of these models which offends the sensitivities of caring Christians. Sometimes they are artificial and unnatural. Many Christians have personal objections to some of the approaches to "winning" the lost. Gimmicks, pseudo-questionnaires, button-holing, evangelical mugging, and the outright rudeness of some witnesses turn them off . . . . Sometimes the only exposure to evangelism for believers is being part of a weekly task force on a "spiritual safari" into enemy territory.

Life-Style Evangelism by Joseph C. Aldrich, pp. 18–19

Choose Sides

Bill and Mary

As Bill and Mary drove home from their first session of a church school class on witnessing, they had a lot to discuss. The leader had asked all class members to make a list of non-Christian friends and acquaintances—and for Bill and Mary that was no easy task. After a great deal of thought, Bill came up with two names, Mary with one.

It wasn't that Bill and Mary weren't friendly. They had lived in Prospect all their lives. They had dozens of friends and relatives—but almost all of them were Christians. In fact, most people in Prospect attended church regularly.

After glancing at the lists, the leader challenged Bill and Mary to expand their number of non-Christian contacts. Other class members offered suggestions too—but they didn't seem especially helpful. As Bill and Mary pulled into their driveway, they were feeling hopeless about their prospects of serving as witnesses for Christ.

That week Bill remembered something. His company was asking for volunteers to work in the central office one thousand miles away. Bill and Mary enjoyed living in Prospect and had never before considered the possibility of moving. They were glad their preschool daughter had such close ties with her grandmas and grandpas, aunts and uncles. But after Sunday's witnessing class, Bill was ready to consider his company's offer. Such a move, he told Mary, would give them a great opportunity to develop contacts among non-Christians in an area that was not as heavily churched as Prospect. "I think the Holy Spirit wants us to move," he said.

Mary was not convinced. She was reluctant to break off close family ties and move away from a community she had known and loved all of her life. She was certain God would not tell them to establish a new home elsewhere for the sake of a more effective witness.

▶Who's right—Bill or Mary? Why?

John and Sue

John worked for a national firm that required him to move to a new location every few years. John and his wife Sue enjoyed the new faces, challenges, and opportunities that such moves provided, but they missed the chance to develop significant long-term relationships with neighbors. As a result, they felt handicapped in their attempts to witness.

Because John and Sue believed they needed deeper ties with their neighbors before they could witness effectively to them, John decided to forgo a promotion in order to establish roots and begin neighboring in earnest. John and Sue were convinced that since Jesus himself asked that we place him above family and earthly circumstances, witness ought to have their highest priority.

▶Did John and Sue reach the right conclusion? Why or why not?

Ways to Make Contacts

Prepare a list of ways you can initiate first-time contacts or strengthen your friendships.

- Plan a neighborhood barbecue or picnic.
- Ask neighbors to your house for dinner or dessert.
- Attend a sporting event or go to the beach together.
- Share a table with someone in the lunchroom at school or at work.
- Join a fraternal or charitable organization.

- _____

- _____

- _____

- _____

- _____

Case Studies

Describe what should be done to strengthen the relationship described in each of the following case studies*:

▶1. George Woods lives a few houses down the street from you. You first met him six months ago when a fire truck rolled up, siren wailing, in front of another neighbor's house. George rushed over to you and asked what had happened. As you watched the firefighters douse the small kitchen fire, you chatted together. George told you he works for an electronics firm and that he and his wife, Marsha, have two teenagers.

▶2. Marsha Woods is George's wife. You met her one evening three months ago when she came to your door soliciting for the March of Dimes. And you discovered that she's quite a talker. She told you that since George's promotion last year he works late and acts as if his office is more important than his family. As a result, she's "going crazy around the house." George is always at work, and the kids are either in school or out with their friends. Marsha claimed she was thinking of finding a job.

▶3. Bill Fisher is in one of your classes at school. He seems friendly, although you've never really talked to him. Bill is tall and lanky and shy. You've seen him several times at the Student Union, slouching at a table alone, reading a book and sipping a Coke.

---

*These case studies are adapted from *Lifestyle Evangelism and Follow-up: A Navigator Video Seminar for the Church*, p. 23.

REFLECTIONS

Preparing a Friendship List

Think about all the people in your life—family, neighbors, friends, coworkers, community servants, associates from committees and guilds, faces you encounter regularly in the park or the supermarket. Many of them are Christians. Some you're not certain about. Others are admittedly non-Christians.

God has put each of these people in your life for a reason. Some will help strengthen your faith. Others need your help in turning to Christ. Without being judgmental—since none of us can judge the true nature of another person's relationship with God—think about the people you know who don't go to church, who don't seem to reflect Christ in the way they speak or act, or who vocally oppose Christ and his church. List their initials in one of the five columns below.

1. Family Members. Include teenage and adult members of your family who seem to be unconvinced about Christ and the church.
2. Neighbors. Include only those who live in your immediate area.
3. Colleagues. Obviously you don't have regular contact with everyone at work or at school. Include only those you know reasonably well or cooperate with directly on work projects, athletic teams, and so forth.
4. Acquaintances. Include people you see frequently at the gas station, at Rotary Club meetings, at Little League baseball games, and so forth.
5. Close Friends. Include those who you know to be non-Christians or unchurched.

1. Family Members

_____

_____

_____

_____

2. Neighbors

_____

_____

_____

_____

3. Colleagues

_____

_____

_____

_____

4. Acquaintances

_____

_____

_____

_____

5. Close friends

_____

_____

_____

_____

Personal Challenge

If you were unable to list at least twelve names, think about some ways in which you can make some new contacts—and some new friends.

Black Like Me

In October 1959, John Howard Griffin visited a doctor, changed his skin pigment to black, and traveled the Deep South.

A veteran political reporter, Griffin had tried all conventional means to understand black culture. None of them had satisfied him.

From November 6 to December 14 Griffin hitchhiked and rode buses through Mississippi, Alabama, Louisiana, and Georgia.

October 28, 1959. For years the idea had haunted me, and that night it returned more insistent than ever. If a white man became a black man in the Deep South, what adjustments would he have to make? What is it like to experience discrimination based on skin color, something over which one has no control?

This speculation was sparked again by a report that lay on my desk. The report mentioned the rise in suicide tendency among Southern blacks. This did not mean that they killed themselves, but rather that they had reached a stage where they simply no longer cared whether they lived or died . . . .

I lingered on in my office. My wife and children slept in our home five miles away. I sat there, surrounded by the smells of autumn coming through my open window, unable to leave, unable to sleep.

How else except by becoming black could a white man hope to learn the truth? . . .

I decided I would do this.

I prepared to walk into a life that appeared suddenly mysterious and frightening. With my decision to become black, I realized that I, a specialist in race issues, really knew nothing of the black's real problem. . . .

On November 1, 1959, John Howard Griffin arrived in New Orleans, Louisiana. There he contacted a dermatologist who prescribed a medication and the use of ultra-violet rays to change Griffin's skin color. By November 7 his skin color had changed to brown, and Griffin entered the world as a black man.

November 21. Three days in Mobile. I spent them walking through the town, searching for jobs. . . . An important part of my daily life was spent searching for the basic things that all whites take for granted: a place to eat, or somewhere to find a drink of water, a rest room, somewhere to wash my hands. . . . I walked into drugstores where a black could buy cigarettes or anything else except soda fountain service. I asked politely where I might find a glass of water. Though they had water not three yards away, they carefully directed me to the nearest black cafe. Had I asked outright for a drink, they would perhaps have given it. But I never asked. Blacks dread rejection, and I waited for them to offer the drink. Not one ever did. . . .

It makes no sense, but in so far as blacks are concerned, nothing makes much sense. This was brought home to me . . . many times when I sought jobs. . . .

I walked through the streets of Mobile throughout the afternoons. I had known the city before, in my youth. . . . It had impressed me as a beautiful Southern port town, gracious and calm. . . . Now, walking the same streets as a black, I found no trace of the Mobile I formerly knew, nothing familiar. . . . The gracious Southerner, the wise Southerner, the kind Southerner was nowhere visible. . . . The atmosphere of a place is entirely different for black and white. The black sees and reacts differently not because he is black, but because he is suppressed. Fear dims even the sunlight. . . .

On November 24, Griffin, hitchhiking through Alabama, was picked up by a black man. The man invited Griffin to spend the night in his two-room house. There Griffin met the man's wife and his six children.

Thinking about these things, the bravery of these people attempting to bring up a family decently, their gratitude that none of their children were blind or maimed, their willingness to share their food and shelter with a stranger—the whole thing overwhelmed me. I got up from bed, half-frozen anyway, and stepped outside.

A thin fog blurred the moon. Trees rose as ghostly masses in the diffused light. I sat on an inverted washtub and trembled as its metallic coldness seeped through my pants.

I thought of my daughter, Susie, and of her fifth birthday today, the candles, the cake and party dress; and of my sons in their best suits. They slept now in clean beds in a warm house while their father, a bald-headed old black man, sat in the swamps and wept, holding it in so he would not awaken the black children.

I felt again the black children's lips against mine, so like the feel of my own children's good-night kisses. I saw again their large eyes, guileless, not yet aware that doors into wonderlands of security, opportunity and hope were closed to them.

It was thrown in my face. I saw it not as a white man and not as a black man, but as a human parent. Their children resembled mine in all ways except the superficial one of skin color, as indeed they resembled all children of all humans. Yet this accident, this least important of all qualities, the skin pigment, marked them for inferior status. It became fully terrifying when I realized that if my skin were permanently black, they would unhesitatingly consign my own children to this bean future.

One can scarcely conceive the full horror of it unless one is a parent who takes a close look at his children and then asks himself how he would feel if a group of men should come to his door and tell him they had decided—for reasons of convenience to them—that his children's lives would henceforth be restricted, their world smaller, their educational opportunities less, their future mutilated.

One would then see it as the black parent sees it, for this is precisely what happens. He looks at his children and knows. No one, not even a saint, can live without a sense of personal value. . . . It is the least obvious but most heinous of all race crimes, for it kills the spirit and the will to live.

It was too much. Though I was experiencing it, I could not believe it. Surely in America a whole segment of decent souls could not stand by and allow such massive crimes to be committed. . . .

When all the talk, all the propaganda has been cut away, the criterion is nothing but the color of skin. My experience proved that. They judged me by no other quality. My skin was dark. That was sufficient reason for them to deny me those rights and freedoms without which life loses its significance and becomes a matter of little more than animal survival. . . .

The next morning Griffin was driven to a small-town bus station where he bought a ticket to Montgomery and waited for the bus to arrive.

How to View People

As I sat in the sunlight, a great heaviness came over me. I went inside to the black rest room, splashed cold water on my face and brushed my teeth. Then I brought out my hand mirror and inspected myself. I had been a black more than three weeks and it no longer shocked me to see the stranger in the mirror. . . .

I noted, too, that my face had lost animation. In repose, it had taken on the strained, disconsolate expression that is written on the countenance of so many Southern blacks. My mind had become the same way, dozing empty for long periods. It thought of food and water, but so many hours were spent just waiting, cushioning self against dread, that it no longer thought of much else. Like the others in my condition, I was finding life too burdensome. . . .

Arriving in Montgomery, Alabama, Griffin encountered a new atmosphere among the city's black citizens.

The blacks' feeling of utter hopelessness is here replaced by a determined spirit of passive resistance. . . . Nonviolent and prayerful resistance to discrimination is the keynote. Here, the black has committed himself to a definite stand. He will go to jail, suffer any humiliation, but he will not back down. He will take the insults and abuses stoically so that his children will not have to take them in the future. . .

If some spark does set the keg afire, it will be a senseless tragedy of ignorant against ignorant, injustice answering injustice—a holocaust that will drag down the innocent and right-thinking masses of human beings.

Then we will all pay for not having cried for justice long ago.

excerpts from *Black Like Me* by John Howard Griffin

To a certain extent, your attitude will be shaped beforehand, determined by the motivating force which lies behind your desire to be involved in evangelism. If the principle driving force comes from the need to add more members to your church, then that will soon become apparent as the number one reason for your call. The same thing will happen if you are primarily interested in your personal fame as an evangelist, a reputation which will be enhanced if you can give a glowing report of a successful visit. In either case, you will be on center stage in your mind's eye while the others are in the wings, waiting for the opportune moment in which they will be called out to play their role. This attitude will become obvious to the discerning host before too long, and it could tear apart the fragile bond which has begun to form.

The development of the proper attitude requires that you see the individual through God's eyes, as one of his children whom Christ has redeemed, as a person who was created to be a part of a loving Father's plan for this world and the next. As you view people from the divine perspective you will soon find that the nonessentials are being filtered out, and that your gaze is left fixed upon that which is all-important. Such things as adding to the church membership rolls or acquiring personal acclaim will fade into insignificance, and in place of these you will find the spotlight focused clearly and intently on that person to whom God has led you.

Agape Evangelism—Roots that Reach Out by
Richard G. Korthals, p. 41

Interpreting Needs

We must not wait until we are healed first, loved first, and then reach out. We must serve no matter how little we have our act together. It may well be that one of the first steps toward our own healing will come when we reach out to someone else. When we get beneath the surface of a person, we will usually discover a sea of needs. We must learn how to interpret those needs correctly, as Jesus did. Jesus wasn't turned off by needs—even needs wrongly met—because they revealed something about the person.

The Samaritan woman had had five husbands and was currently living with a sixth man. The disciples took one look at her and felt, "That woman? Become a Christian? No way, why just look at her lifestyle!" But Jesus looked at her and came to the opposite conclusion. What Jesus saw in her frantic male-hopping wasn't just looseness. It wasn't her human need for tenderness that alarmed him, but rather how she sought to meet that need. Even more, Jesus saw that her need indicated hunger for God. He seemed to be saying to the disciples, "Look at what potential she has for God. See how hard she's trying to find the right thing in all the wrong places."

That blows the lid right off evangelism for me. How many Samaritan men and women do you know? Everywhere I am, I see people frantically looking for the right things in all the wrong places. The tragedy is that so often my initial response is to withdraw and assume they will never become Christians. We must ask ourselves, "How do I interpret the needs and lifestyles of my friends?"

Out of the Saltshaker by Rebecca M. Pippert, p. 119

The Motive for Evangelism

Which love for neighbors must motivate him who would bring the evangel to the unsaved is not difficult to say. That love which is the product of common grace alone is quite insufficient, for it will seek the temporal and material good of men, but hardly their spiritual and eternal welfare. That love which is restricted to friends is utterly inadequate, for the bearer of the gospel must love those who persecute him and pray for them, as did the Lord Jesus when he pleaded for those who were nailing him to the cross: "Father, forgive them; for they know not what they do" (Luke 23:34), and as Stephen did when he interceded for those who were stoning him to death: "Lord, lay not this sin to their charge" (Acts 7:60). And, obviously, that love for man which is divorced from love for God and co-exists with hatred of God cannot possibly serve as a motive for proclaiming the gospel of the grace of God. Only he who has been born of the Spirit of God, who loves his neighbors because he loves God, who loves his enemies, blesses them that curse him, does good to them that hate him, prays for them which despitefully use him and persecute him, and thus manifests himself to be a child of the heavenly Father (Matt. 5:44–45), has the proper motive for offering the Christ of the gospel to sinful men.

God-Centered Evangelism by R. B. Kuiper, p. 87

TWO

FRIENDSHIPS

Sometimes witnessing seems easy. We can all think of times in a distant airport or at the local supermarket when God gave us a quick providential opportunity to talk about our faith with someone. We should thank God for experiences like that—for the occasional bolt from the blue that spices up our lives. But then it's time to get back to work.

Ordinarily non-Christians come to God not by a chance encounter but through long-term friendship with believers: those outside the faith are *first* attracted to Christians and *then* to Christ.

That doesn't mean we should make friends with the idea of "capturing" them for Christ, or that we should view the non-Christians we encounter as spiritual projects. We should seek rapport, look for common ground, and get into the needs of others because we love them. Certainly we should sharpen our verbal skills and capitalize on the connections that develop along the way. But the reaping mentality is always bathed in love. Our goal is to build a network of shared experiences. Our heart's desire must be maintaining friendships—even if those friends never decide for Christ.

In *Life-Style Evangelism*, Joseph Aldrich defines evangelism as "living beautifully and opening one's web of friendships to include the nonbeliever." Friendship is the basis and the aim. Using our people eyes, we make contacts and take the first step in creating friendships. With our friends we can credibly share the claims of Christ. A witness is a friend-maker for God.

Bible Study: Mark 2:15–17

▶1. "Why does he eat with tax collectors and 'sinners'?" asked the Pharisees. They were, in effect, asking why Jesus was associating with known cheats and with outcasts of every kind, including the immoral. Who are the "tax collectors and sinners" of today?

▶2. During Christ's time, the dinner table was a place of intimate fellowship. Jesus used mealtimes to socialize with those whom the Pharisees despised. In what ways do we relate to the "tax collectors and sinners" of our world?

▶3. A cardinal principle of friendship is to avoid judging, condemning, or moralizing. We are to demonstrate grace, not legalism. It is the Holy Spirit's responsibility to convict of sin, not ours (John 16:8–11). "No thank you" is definitely better than "I don't drink because I'm a Christian and the Bible says . . . ." Praying before lunch may embarrass—not edify—your non-Christian guest. Do you agree with this principle and with the suggested strategies? In light of 1 Corinthians 9:19–23 and Mark 2:15–17, why or why not?

While Jesus was having dinner at Levi's house, many tax collectors and "sinners" were eating with him and his disciples, for there were many who followed him. When the teachers of the law who were Pharisees saw him eating with the "sinners" and tax collectors, they asked his disciples: "Why does he eat with tax collectors and 'sinners'?" On hearing this, Jesus said to them, "It is not the healthy who need a doctor, but the sick. I have not come to call the righteous, but sinners.

Mark 2:15–17

Friendship Index

How deep are your friendships with those you'd like to witness to? The "Friendship Index" will help you determine that. Use the index to rate the depth of your relationships with the person you listed in chapter 1. Simply put the person's initials in the proper box for each of the six categories (job, interests, cultural background, etc.)

Assigning a person a *1* for a given category indicates that you know almost nothing about him or her in that category; a *2* indicates some general knowledge, and a *3* indicates very specific, detailed knowledge.

Obviously being a friend involves more than *knowing* many things about a person. It involves trust and rapport and many other ingredients that take time and care to develop. However, the amount we know about a person is often a good indicator of how deep our friendship is. If you score a majority of *1s* on the Friendship Index, you'll not have many opportunities to talk about Christ.

	1 Know almost nothing	2 Know in general	3 Know great detail
Job, present and past, including future aspirations	▶	▶	▶
Interests, hobbies, sports, likes, dislikes	▶	▶	▶
Cultural, ethnic, religious background	▶	▶	▶
Problems, needs (physical and emotional)	▶	▶	▶
Personality traits. What makes the person sad, content; fears, worries, greatest thrills	▶	▶	▶
Leisure time, friends, possessions	▶	▶	▶

Based on this system, score your top twelve contacts:

Initials	Score
1. _____	_____
2. _____	_____
3. _____	_____
4. _____	_____
5. _____	_____
6. _____	_____
7. _____	_____
8. _____	_____
9. _____	_____
10. _____	_____
11. _____	_____
12. _____	_____

How did you do? If you scored 15 or more points for any one person you rated, you've probably already had an opportunity to witness to him or her.

One or two of the persons you rated the highest should receive your special attention in the near future. But also consider ways to get better acquainted with those contacts you rated lower.

Deepening Friendships

Making friendships work is easier for some Christians than for others. A few of us have the knack and sensitivity for putting people at ease. Some of us are fun to be with. But no matter what our gifts, friendships don't just happen spontaneously.

Listed below are some ABCs of friend-making. Read over the suggestions carefully, noting in the margin those you have tried or would feel comfortable trying.

a. Refer to facts from earlier conversations (not mechanically, but showing true concern). Remember details; store them away and write them down when you get home. Without notes we forget 50 percent within twenty-four hours.

b. Unless they are showing obvious signs of feeling pressured, continue to invite people to your home—even if they don't reciprocate.

c. Tell them you'll be on the lookout for anything they've expressed a need for—a job opening, for example, or a used car. Keep your promise.

d. Follow up on an illness or unresolved problem with a telephone call or a quick visit.

e. Send a card, flowers, or other thoughtful communication when a person is experiencing personal illness or death in the family.

f. Stop by on a summer evening—but don't overstay your welcome. Remember Proverbs 25:17: "Seldom set foot in your neighbor's house—too much of you, and he will hate you."

g. Suggest that their children come and play with yours.

h. Listen patiently and sympathize with their problems. Don't rush in and tell them what to do. Share their burden with them.

i. Go together to a sporting event, a concert, a dinner, a movie.

j. Adopt some of their interests. Enjoy them as people and let them enjoy you.

k. Don't recoil at unregenerate behavior or language. You can accept people while not condoning all their actions.

l. Share your interests, problems, frustrations.

m. Invite them to attend worship or a church-sponsored activity with you.

n. Lend them a book that might help them through a crisis or answer a particular need.

o. Make yourself available to help them with a project.

Lifestyle Evangelism and Follow-up: A Navigator Video Seminar for the Church, p. 42

Alice Miller's rule of thumb is a good one: "If it is very painful for you to criticize your friends, you are safe doing it. But if you take the slightest pleasure in it, that is the time to hold your tongue."

The Friendship Factor by Alan Loy McGinnis, p. 68

The Gospel Blimp

The idea really began that night several years ago when we were all sitting around in George and Ethel Griscom's backyard.

We'd just finished eating an outdoor picnic supper (a real spread), and there wasn't much to do except swat mosquitoes and watch the fireflies. Every so often an airplane flew over, high in the sky. You could see the twinkling red and white lights.

I guess that's what got us started on the Gospel Blimp. Or maybe it was George and Ethel's next-door neighbors, who were playing cards and drinking beer on the porch.

Anyway, we began talking about how to reach people with the gospel. Herm's active in the local businessmen's group. So when we started talking about reaching people, Herm says, "Let's take those folks next door to you, George, for example. You can tell they're not Christians. Now if we wanted to give them the gospel, how'd we . . ."

"Herm, for goodness' sake, keep your voice down," Marge interrupted. "D'you want them to hear you?"

"Herm's right, they're not Christians," George agreed. "Go to church—a liberal one—Christmas and Easter. But drink and play cards most other Sundays. Except the summer. In a few weeks they'll start going to the shore each weekend until Labor Day."

"O.K. now. Any suggestions?" Herm is a good discussion leader.

"Hey, look at that plane. It's really low. You can almost see the lights in the windows . . ."

"Like I was saying, here's a test. How do we go about giving the gospel to those people over there?" And Herm motioned toward the house next door.

"Too bad that plane didn't carry a sign. They looked up from their card playing long enough to have read it if it had carried one."

"Hey, you know you may have something there. Any of you seen those blimps with signs trailing on behind? You know, 'Drink Pepsi Cola,' or 'Chevrolet is First'? . . . What I mean is this. Why not have a blimp with a Bible verse trailing—something like 'Believe on the Lord Jesus Christ and thou shalt be saved.' "

"I can see it now. The world's first vertical blimp, straight up and down like that tree. Anchored by a sign."

"Stop making fun. We could get a shorter verse."

"Sounds like a terrific idea. Really terrific. Why, everybody would get the gospel at the same time."

"Everybody except blind people and children who aren't able to read."

"Nothing's perfect. Anyway it does sound terrific, like Marge said."

"How'd we go about it? And wouldn't it be awfully expensive? I mean, buying the blimp, and blowing it up, and everything."

"Hey, it's time for the Maxie Belden show."

"Aw, who wants to watch TV on a night like this, stars and breeze and all. Well, if everybody else is going inside . . ."

———————

I guess we'd have left it at that—just one of those crazy things you talk about when a group gets together for supper and the evening—if it hadn't been for Herm. . . .

The next Thursday Herm brought the idea to our weekly businessman's luncheon. . . . Herm summarized the Gospel Blimp idea. He really did a good job. You could just tell that different ones were getting excited as he talked. Nobody even

started on their ice cream until he was through.

"And so I suggest," Herm ended, in a real loud voice, "that we appoint a committee. Maybe it's for the birds. Maybe not. But anyway," and here he paused and looked around the room again, "we ought to be reaching people somehow. . . ."

That afternoon we were a little late ending the luncheon, but by the time we did, a committee had been formed. With Herm as chairman.

"All you fellows on the committee, stay behind a few minutes," Herm called out above the scraping of the chairs as we rose to go. "We'll have to settle on a meeting time. This'll take work—lots of it."

———————

I stopped at Griscoms' to return George's power drill. I'd been getting the P.A. system ready to install on the blimp. So I asked Ethel about their neighbors.

"Nothing new," she says. "I mean, nothing to get excited about as far as their salvation is concerned. But she hasn't been well. I think they took her to the hospital two or three days ago. We can see him eating over there alone at night. And always a bottle of beer. Sometimes two."

"What hospital's she in?" I asked.

"I don't know. I'll tell George you stopped with the drill. By the way, how's the sound system coming? . . . Will people really be able to hear it?"

"With a hundred watts output? And three cone speakers? Listen, they'll be able to hear it anywhere—even in a basement. No worry about that."

"The Women's Auxiliary is really thrilled about the sound system. You know we've been concerned about blind people, and children who can't read yet, and people who are near-sighted. And people who can't get outside to see the blimp, like invalids, and old men and women in convalescent homes, and people in hospitals. It'll be comforting to know we're doing something for them."

"Well, tell George I stopped. And thanks for the drill."

———————

When we started using the P.A. system on the flying blimp about a week later, a new epoch in the blimp's ministry began. In a sense, it seemed to give final assurance that the total evangelization of our little city was a distinct possibility. . . .

I'll never forget the first night. I had gone down to the drugstore to get a box of candy and a card (having been reminded during dessert that it was our wedding anniversary), when suddenly I heard it.

In loud tones, on the wings of the night as it were, came the sound of "Rolled away, rolled away, rolled away, every burden of my heart rolled away." Honest, it was tremendous.

People came out of houses, cars stopped, everybody tried to figure where it was coming from.

Of course, I knew. For I had put the last Phillips screw through the third speaker only that afternoon. But the rest of the people were puzzled because the blimp was nowhere in sight.

Next came a vibraharp rendition of the Glory Song, followed by about fifty kids singing the Hash Chorus. But it wasn't until the music had stopped and the Commander's voice came on, "Now hear this, all you people," that the blimp hove in sight. It wasn't full moon, but it was still bright enough to see the blimp clearly outlined against the sky.

I suppose the Commander preached about ten minutes the first time. Or maybe it took ten minutes for the blimp to get out of earshot. But even though it was short, he was able to get in two invitations. The vibraharp came on for a few bars of "Almost Persuaded" each time. . . .

I tell you, I was really thrilled. When I got home with the candy, I phoned up Griscoms to tell them the good news.

"I know why you're calling," says George before I have a chance to tell him. "Listen." And he holds the phone away from his head. In the background, coming through clear as a bell, I can hear, "Hallelu, Hallelu, Hallelu."

Were we ever enthused. I think, looking back, that night was the high point of the whole blimp project. . . .

excerpts from The Gospel Blimp by Joseph Bayly, pp. 9–13, 28–30

After reading this story, discuss the two questions, below:

▶1. What does this parable tell us about evangelism?

▶2. Do you agree with one of Bayly's own conclusions:

"One great factor is our North American demand for bigness. We must increase the budget, employ more workers, nationalize (better yet, internationalize) the scope of our activities, acquire more property, take over more elaborate physical facilities: these are our Christian status symbols. And not merely status on a human level, for divine status as well is proved by these signs of outward prosperity. Financial provision for an enlarging program is usually considered the prime evidence that a Christian work is proceeding according to the will of God."

REFLECTIONS

Mario

A Brazilian friend, Mario, and I studied the Bible for four years together before he became a Christian. As an intellectual who had read almost all of the leading Western thinkers from Rousseau to Kafka, he had blended a personal philosophy with Bertrand Russell as his patron saint. He was a political activist, a leader in many Marxist activities. Why he kept studying the Bible with me for four years, or why I stuck with him so long, neither of us can explain today. But there we were.

Since he lived life on the philosophical plane, our Bible studies were often pitched in that direction. One day, a couple of years after Mario had become a Christian, he and I were reminiscing. He asked me, "Do you know what it really was that made me decide to become a Christian?" Of course, I immediately thought of our numerous hours of Bible study, but I responded, "No, what?"

His reply took me completely by surprise. He said, "Remember that first time I stopped by your house? We were on our way someplace together and I had a bowl of soup with you and your family. As I sat there observing you, your wife, your children, and how you related to each other, I asked myself, When will I have a relationship like this with my fiancee? When I realized the answer was 'never,' I concluded I had to become a Christian for the sake of my own survival."

I remembered the occasion well enough to recall that our children were not particularly well-behaved that evening. In fact, I remembered I had felt frustrated when I corrected them in Mario's presence.

Our family was unaware of our influence on Mario. God had done this work through our family without our knowing it.

Evangelism as a Lifestyle by Jim Petersen, pp. 18–19

▶ What conclusions can you reach from this example? Is this a typical example, do you think, or is it somewhat unusual?

REFLECTIONS

Committees

The jokes we make about committees are often deserved . . . . A committee keeps minutes and wastes hours. The most effective committee is made up of three people, one of whom is sick, and the other out of town. A committee is a way of postponing a decision. A committee is a group of people who individually can do nothing and who collectively decide nothing can be done . . . . Yet, when all is said and done, what would we do without them.

It is well, upon occasion, to peruse the backs of church bulletins, to see the committees listed there, and to breathe a twofold word of thanks: first of all, gratitude for their existence; and second, thanksgiving for the fact that John 3:16 reads the way it does. For God so loved the world that He didn't send a committee.

Of Cabbages and Kings by Jacob D. Eppinga, pp. 104–105

Give Specific Invitations

A broader aspect of our social involvement with non-Christians is the whole question of inviting them into our homes. We often think, "I don't have anything in common with a non-Christian"; then we're stymied. If we share no interests at all, why get together and have a flop? We're afraid he'll be bored if he joins us in some activity with him. This dilemma is easily solved by planning what we'll do together beforehand. Instead of just saying, "Joe, can you come over Tuesday evening?" or "I'm having several of the students home for the weekend. Can you come?" we can specifically suggest, "to play ping pong?" or "to go skiing?" This solves the "What shall we do?" problem at the outset. The person who's being invited knows what to expect; if he's not interested, he can decline the invitation without embarrassing anyone. But nine times out of ten, he'll want to come.

We also need to think about secondary issues that arise in our relationships with a group. Many of our group associations are by necessity rather than preference. Since we don't choose the other members of the group, they seldom consider our individual behavior as a personal affront to them. Individual feelings aren't hurt as easily in a group as they are in a personal relationship. In the group, therefore, we can do things that on a personal basis we would hesitate to do for fear of condemning the friend.

How to Give Away Your Faith by Paul Little, p. 51

Express Love

In all of these secondary issues, a little advance thought now can prevent much embarrassment. We aren't devising gimmicks to get at people with the gospel surreptitiously. We're seeking ways of expressing the love of Jesus Christ. Because the Lord has come into our lives, our capacity to love is deepening. His love is being shed abroad in our hearts to be poured out for others. We love people for themselves, as total men rather than abstractions. If Jesus Christ is a personal reality to us, His love will reach out through us to some very unlovely people whom everyone else despises; He gives us the capacity to love them as people.

As one expression of our love for them, we want to communicate the gospel. But no friendship should depend on how the other person responds to the gospel. Unfortunately, many non-Christians today are suspicious of all Christians because of a previous contact with a friendly religious person who had ulterior motives. Some non-Christians refuse to listen to a single word about our Lord until they're sure we'll be their friends regardless—even if they reject Jesus Christ. We must love each person for himself.

How to Give Away Your Faith by Paul Little, p. 52

Afraid?

A lot of our fear that people are going to reject us and react negatively is just a preconceived idea in our minds.

The fact is that most people, if approached in a natural and sensitive way, will react with politeness and interest. Surprisingly, many have been waiting for someone to come. The way God has prepared them may not be as dramatic as Saul of Tarsus. But there are many persons around us who are dealt with through loneliness, bereavement, family crisis, sickness, concern about the world, search for purpose, or the need for forgiveness. Much of our fear will be gone if we realize that God will often lead us to those whose hearts he is ready to open.

The best antidote to fear is love—a love that leads us to forget our own fears and focus on the needs of others. Perhaps that's why Paul wrote to Timothy, apparently a sometimes hesitant type, to remind him that "God did not give us a spirit of timidity, but a spirit of power, of love, and of self-discipline" (2 Tim. 1:7).

God's love will not only cast out fear, it will transform our witnessing from compulsion to compassion.

Good News Is For Sharing by Leighton Ford, p. 21

REFLECTIONS

Nothing in Common?

Frequently the unsaved are viewed as enemies rather than victims of the Enemy. Spirituality is viewed as separation from the unsaved. The new Christian is told he has "nothing in common" with his unsaved associates. Quite frankly, I have a lot in common with them: a mortgage, car payments, kids who misbehave, a lawn to mow, a car to wash, a less-than-perfect marriage, a few too many pounds around my waist, and an interest in sports, hobbies, and other activities they enjoy. It is well to remember that Jesus was called a "friend of sinners." A *friend* of sinners. Selah!

Life-Style Evangelism by Joseph C. Aldrich, p. 28

A Proper View of Separation

In order to work with unsaved people, one must have *a healthy understanding of separation.* Separation is not maintaining a "radical difference" and avoiding "radical identification." A position between radical difference and identification must be maintained as a system of checks and balances. Biblical separation is not simply avoiding a negative (sin). The believer is to be separated *from* sin and separated *unto* God. Separation is not isolation from unredeemed mankind; rather it is separation from acts of personal sin and separation unto God.

Some churches today are similar to a department store where all the employees arrive at the prescribed time, lock the doors, and then sell merchandise to each other all day. To do any good, salt has to not only get out of the shaker, but it must come into contact with the food. Otherwise, it's useless.

Life-Style Evangelism by Joseph C. Aldrich, p. 189

THREE

OPENINGS

We witness most effectively when we use natural bridges to let others know we belong to God. Instead of barging in and announcing who we are and what we stand for, we witness on those occasions when it makes sense to tell people who we are: "We're praying for your mother." "God has really blessed our country." "I respect that person because he is created in God's image." All such comments open doors for our non-Christian friends to enter.

As our friendships grow and deepen, we will discover more and more natural bridges for talking about our ultimate concerns. And it's important that we use them. The same Paul who stressed the sweet incense of life-style also reminds us that no one will hear the good news unless those who are sent talk about it (Rom. 10:14–15). The more skilled we are in conversation the better we represent the Kingdom to which we belong.

As Spirit-led Christians, then, we must live distinctively, always looking for opportunities for verbal witness. Both our actions and our words should show our non-Christian friends how a Christian thinks and how a Christian acts.

Leading Questions

Below are typical questions that you might inject into a conversation to turn it to spiritual concerns. Have you used any of them effectively? What others would you recommend?

James W. Fowler, author of *Stages of Faith* has developed an excellent set of general questions:

▶1. Do you consider yourself a religious person? Why or why not?

▶2. Do you have, or have you had, experiences you might call religious? Please explain.

▶3. When you think of God, what associations and feelings do you have?

▶4. Are there specific events or experiences in your past or present life that might help me understand why you think about God in these ways?

▶5. At present, what gives your life meaning and purpose?

▶6. Is there a "growing edge" in your life right now? Does something in your life need to change in order to make it more full or complete? Please explain.

Other recommended questions include the following:

▶1. Which of the religious leaders of the world do you know most about? Buddha, Mohammed, Jesus, or someone else? Where did you learn about this leader?

▶2. According to your understanding, who is Jesus Christ?

▶3. Do you ever worry about death?

▶4. In your opinion, how does a person become a Christian?

▶5. Someone told me the other day that since everyone cheats a little, it doesn't make sense to be totally honest. "Why should I be so righteous?" he said. What do you think about his conclusions?

▶6. In a recent Gallup poll more than 90 percent of those interviewed said they believed in God. Do you think this statistic is accurate?

▶7. Of all the social problems facing us today, which one do you think is most critical? What do you view as the primary cause of this problem?

▶8. When a person talks with you about a problem, ask: "What solution would you suggest? Have you considered Christianity as a possible answer?"

Additional leading questions that you (and others) can suggest:

▶1.

▶2.

▶3.

The Christian faculty members at a state university recently published the following half-page ad in the school newspaper. As a strategy for initiating conversations, how do you rate its value? Could something similar be posted on the bulletin board in a factory or distributed through a company newsletter or elsewhere? Would you want your name in such an ad? Why or why not?

An Invitation from Christian Faculty

We whose names appear below are a few of the Christians teaching, doing research, and working in other capacities on this campus. Our names and home phones are listed to indicate that we shall be happy to discuss issues of Christian faith and life with any who are interested.

We have great respect for the necessary neutrality of the classroom, laboratory, and studio, for we understand how inquiry must incorporate doubt while avoiding prejudice and how teaching must be sensitive to a diversity of points of view. Yet we understand also that young people in their college years are examining value-systems and religious positions with an eye to determining the larger goods to which they will devote their lives.

We have confirmed for ourselves that the call to new life which Jesus gave nearly two thousand years ago remains relevant today. His call is startling in its simplicity, its rigor, and its promise: "He who finds his life will lose it, and he who loses his life for my sake will find it. . . . Take my yoke upon you, and learn from me, for I am gentle and lowly in heart, and you will find rest for your souls" (Matt. 10:39; 11:29).

Jesus' words serve to remind us that learning may involve much more than inquiry. The learning that takes place in the framework of discipleship is vital to the full flowering of the human person.

Gary Achtemeier State Water Survey 352-1387	**Jack Everly** Agricultural Communications 344-5738	**R.E. Klien** Mechanical Engineering 1-586-3759	**Jack Pullen** Geology 351-8361
Wendell Anderson Adult Education 367-5263	**William C. Gamble** Civil Engineering 384-1461	**Samuel Lanford** Architecture 352-5330	**Donald Queller** History 356-7560
David H. Baker Animal Science 359-4789	**Gilbert R. Hollis** Animal Science 359-9418	**Robert McColley** History 344-5138	**Robert Sutton** History 344-4644
Richard Boileau Physical Education 352-1264	**Aldon Jensen** Animal Science 367-3694	**Daniel Offner** Mechanical Engineering 367-4440	**Robert Wilhelmson** Atmospheric Sciences 1-586-1731
Vernon Burton History 337-1511	**U. Milo Kaufmann** English 328-1770	**David Opperman** Engineering 367-9430	**Eugene Ziegler** Agronomy 367-7156

Bible Study: Sermon on the Mount

In the first passage Jesus instructs us to let others see our good deeds—not to bring glory to ourselves but to motivate others to praise God. Does the second passage—given in the context of alms-giving, prayer, and fasting—contradict the first? How do you account for the difference between the two passages? How can "doing good deeds" be a positive witness in one instance and a negative witness in another?

In the same way, let your light shine before men, that they may see your good deeds and praise your Father in heaven.
Matthew 5:16

Be careful not to do your 'acts of righteousness' before men, to be seen by them. If you do, you will have no reward from your Father in heaven.
Matthew 6:1

Proud to Bear My Father's Name

In American society, my dad might not rate very high. For it praises brainy, brawny, and handsome men. Who are its idols? None but the intelligent and well-educated, the athletic and muscular, the ruggedly good-looking. How else to explain the mad pursuit among us for a well-tanned, properly exercised physique and clothes "just right for the occasion"? Measured against these fond trifles, my dad's a certain loser. He's not particularly dashing, clever, or sexy: he's only 129 pounds and five feet, five inches tall. And though he wanted to go further in school, he never got beyond the eighth grade. He had to work the family farm.

But by my measure, my dad's a giant of a man, every square inch of him. He often quips, "Ability makes the man and not the size," and in his case it's true—indisputably so.

When he married my mom in 1941, Dad obviously didn't have a ghost of an idea that four short years later some stray polio germ would invade his wife's body and leave it with but a tiny fraction of the vitality it once had—and in the process permanently change the entire course of his life, too. There he was in 1945, a thirty-two-year-old man taught by his father to love the soil and now himself an ambitious onion farmer who had just purchased his first ten acres of land. It was a small beginnning to be sure, but already he was dreaming big. And I'm sure he could have made it big too, for he was a classy farmer who matched ingenuity with hard work.

Then, on a cold November day in 1945 everything changed. No one expected it or could have planned for it, but my mom got sick—and within four days she was totally paralyzed. For the rest of her days she would live in an iron lung—permanently so. And this turn of events put Dad, in the prime of his life, face to face with a decision: What should I do now? Who will care for the kids? (My brother was four months old, and I was four years.) He asked, "What about the crop? The farm? The dreams?"

Given our throwaway society and the standards by which it weighs factors and comes to decisions, I think I know what most men would have done. They would have counted the personal cost, calculated the risk and sacrifice, figured out what was left for them, and promptly quit. For life really does owe them more, they would have reckoned. After all, when deprived of a decent job, a stable income, a healthy wife and kids, what man can really think well of himself, hold his head high, be well adjusted and life affirming? Given the circumstances facing my dad, most men would have rationalized, "The woman now in an iron lung isn't the same person with whom I stood before the marriage altar, so why be bound to her in loyalty now?" In fact, I suspect that most men would judge another as perhaps slightly crazed, and at any rate certainly foolish and stupid, to hang in there with a wife whose glamour and sexiness were now gone, whose ability to entertain, cook, travel, garden, vacation, and work—the routine things husbands enjoy in their wives—had now been taken away. The generation to which I belong would have calculated the factors, lining the assets up alongside the liabilities and figuring out almost mathematically, as it were, whether staying was worth it. Our culture, as everyone knows, massively encourages self-maximizing. The response of a California yuppie to his recent divorce is typical: "There wasn't any cheese in it any longer. So I bagged it."

But my dad didn't. He remembered his expensive vows, and he kept them magnificently. To begin with, he stayed with Mom in the hospital. And not just during visiting hours or a few days or weeks. No, he gave up working the farm and literally lived at the hospital with Mom, day after day, during her four-year stay. Polio patients were routinely isolated from everyone, but in Dad's case the doctor made an exception. He noted the dramatic and medically inexplicable improvement that Dad's presence was making in Mom's condition, and he allowed him free access to the polio ward. He summarized his order to the staff tersely: "Let Mrs. Cooper's husband come in to be by her—whenever." Such permission was unheard of.

Finally Mom could come home from the hospital. And Dad kept on keeping his vows. He held her almost totally in his care. Tending to her needs developed into a routine. Every morning he lifted her from the iron lung and gave her her daily care, washing her, brushing her teeth, combing her hair, rubbing her back, dispensing her medications, and so much more. He was the hands by which she did things: he turned pages in a book or a magazine, he fed her, he switched on the TV, he wrote the Christmas and birthday cards, he did their shopping, he cleaned the house, and so on. Only open heart surgery several years ago kept him, for the first time in some thirty-six years, from daily tending to her.

Not only was my mom my dad's wife. She was also his work. He gave everything to her. And not only physical things but massive doses of encouragement too. Her upbeat and jovial nature was matched and rivaled by his. Never—never—did I see him sullen or morose, despondent or asking why. He was like a Barnabas to her and to us all, an encourager of the rarest class. Without him my mom would never have survived. She was his whole life and he entirely hers. After she died, he said simply and profoundly, if somewhat ungrammatically, "Margie and me, we was just like that." And he clasped his hands together. Never among human beings have I seen such selfless devotion.

But what staggers me the most is that he did all of this so uncomplainingly, as though it were no big deal. Hero though he was, he never considered himself one. Not once did I hear Dad sigh, "Oh, if only I could work and have life like other men." When I asked him recently how he could have made the decision to stay, knowing that doing so would forever alter some of his fondest hopes and dreams, he waved it off with a flick of his hand. "I never even thought of doing anything else. You just do it, and God helps you." My dad had cultivated the habit of keeping a promise.

A few years ago, when my folks celebrated their fortieth wedding anniversary, a local newspaper carried the story. It reported, too, their exceptional family circumstances. Apparently someone thought it newsworthy enough to make the UPI wire service, for soon my folks received news clippings and congratulations from everywhere. I recall one TV newscaster's call from Chicago. "Mr. Cooper," he asked, "is this story true? Has she been sick that long? But also is it really true that you've remained by her side?"

"Yes," replied my dad in almost total surprise at the question. "Well, I can hardly believe it," replied the newsman in astonishment. "You're worth doing a story on, for I can't imagine anyone sticking with his wife when she has so little left to offer." Then my diminutive and slightly ill-at-ease dad, never one to preach a sermon, declared the gospel in an eloquence that I shall never possess. He said, "I love my wife. I'm a Christian, and we try to keep our promises."

Through years of faithfulness my father, now seventy-three, has given me a legacy of what life at its core is really about. For with selfless love he kept his vows and doing so gave God the glory. He taught me what a promise made and kept is really all about. I now publicly thank him for it and consider it a distinct privilege and high honor to bear his name.

"Proud to Bear My Father's Name" by Dale Cooper,
The Banner, June 16, 1986, pp. 8–10

After reading this article, discuss or think about the following questions:

▶1. What do you think of Mr. Cooper's response to the Chicago newscaster? Could you improve on it?

▶2. Give an example from your own experience in which response to illness was a great testimony.

▶3. Take a minute to describe a Christian who has impressed you. Conclude by thinking about some of the qualities that make our lives distinctive.

▶4. How would you respond to the following personal compliments:

    a. "Your children don't seem to have the problems so many other kids have. What have you done for them?

    b. You work hard and are always honest.

    c. You really have an upbeat attitude about life.

    d. I have never heard you criticize anyone, even your wife and children!

REFLECTIONS

A Bridge of Acceptance

How do you build a bridge of acceptance rather than a wall of rejection in a few brief moments? One of the ways is by conveying the idea that your first concern is for each person as an individual, and that all else is of secondary importance. To accomplish this requires the right choice of words and the proper tone of voice, accompanied by facial expressions and mental attitudes which are in accord with the spoken message. In other words, you present or create an image or "link" of love . . . .

Love is frequently thought of as being the intensification of like. *Agape* does not mean that, nor require it. In fact, you can feel *agape* for a person and not "like" him or her at all. God knows that I will not necessarily like all people for that would imply that I would be attracted to every individual, and that just does not happen. Certain types of personalities do attract me, but others have the opposite effect. There are forms of behavior which I find repugnant, and it would be almost impossible for me to like or be attracted to someone associated with that kind of life-style.

When God tells me that I must *"agape,"* or love, that person, he means that I should have a selfless concern for that individual or human being. He also asks me to carefully separate deed from doer. He does not ask me to love the manner of living, but he does ask me to love the human being that does the living.

Agape Evangelism—Roots that Reach Out by Richard G. Korthals, p. 39

Shy?

A girl told me once that she was dreadfully shy. Just the thought of talking to someone terrified her. But she was a committed Christian and knew she had to find ways to reach out. She was perceptive and realized she shouldn't ask God suddenly to make her a boisterous extrovert. Rather she asked him for the freedom to look outward, not to look at herself and be paralyzed by fear. She told me she got a summer job as a waitress because it would force her to talk with people.

When she returned to the university, she applied some newly learned lessons. When she was eating in the cafeteria, she would ask her table, "I'm going back for milk. Can I get anyone anything?" Usually a few would reply yes. When she returned with what they requested, it almost immediately opened up conversation and they asked her questions. She said the fact that they were both focusing on the extra milk she had in her hand reduced her fear of eye-to-eye contact. Her being able to focus on something else (even if it was a piece of pie!) kept her from focusing on herself. That led her on to discovering other ways to serve.

She had a plant that everyone admired. So when someone said she had a beautiful plant, she would say, "Thanks! Let me give you a cutting." That offer opened conversation but kept her focusing initially on the plant, which helped her fears. She has offered to help students preparing for tests if they were in her field or needed a paper typed. Eventually after much practice and continually raising the stakes, she became more and more at ease around people. It was a learned skill. But what freed her and helped her to love and accept herself—and others—was learning that she could take initiative and that people responded to her. She was still reserved but not so desperately afraid. She loved people powerfully but quietly.

Out of the Saltshaker by Rebecca M. Pippert, pp. 122–123

REFLECTIONS

Another Life

Think about the meaning of the following parable. Could you give it to a friend to stimulate his or her curiosity about spiritual matters?

You could measure by the wiggles of Bubu the tadpole's tail, his contempt for tadpoles who couldn't think. His experience as chairman of the Little Pond Philosophical and Debating Society had impressed upon him not only the importance of reason, but also the penetrative ability of his own mind. The reflection encouraged him as he wiggled gently among soft curtains of sunlight in cool green waters.

Powerful thrusts from his vigorous legs propelled a frog to Bubu's side. He was a new member of the Philosophical Society and Bubu greeted him warmly. Though the frog appeared to Bubu to be bound by superstition and subjectivism, he nevertheless showed promise.

"Beautiful day," said Bubu.

"Beautiful," agreed the frog. "And up above it's tremendous. I never knew such colors existed before my conversion."

If Bubu was embarrassed, he gave no sign of it. "I don't mind your sincerity in the least," he murmured smilingly, "though from my reading in psychology, I suspect that your conversion is merely a psychological phenomenon."

The frog looked puzzled. "Well, it's a phenomenon, anyway. I know I'm different from what I was before." He looked at Bubu's quivering tail and then at his own powerful muscles. "For instance, I can do things now that I never used to be able to do."

Bubu grew solemn."You are different because you think you are different. I personally have observed the difference and it confirms all I have come to believe about the overwhelming influence of mind over body."

Something akin to pity filled the frog's eyes as he looked at him. "But Bubu," he said quietly, "the world up above that I talk about is real. I can't explain it, but in a sense it's more real than the watery universe we live in."

"More real *to you*."

"More real to anybody, Bubu."

"But not at all real to me."

The frog had lost his bantering manner entirely. "Bubu, the world would be there whether I could feel it or not. It's still there even though you don't believe it. Right now, as we talk, soft breezes blow across the surface of Little Pond. A burning sun pours rays over the bodies of animals, birds, and plants. Other frogs like me are leaping across dry ground. Bubu, I've seen clouds. I've been warmed by the sun. I—"

The tadpole's annoyance nearly choked him. "Show me!" he cried. "Show me this sun. Show me a piece of dry."

There was a pause, filled only with soft underwater sounds.

"I have to admit," the frog said finally, "that it's impossible for me to show you the sun. If you are to see it, your eyes will have to change. There's a verse in the Sacred Book that says, 'Except a tadpole metamorphose, it cannot see the kingdom of dryness.' I'd like you to see and know what I see and know. I hope one day to take you hopping with me between blades of grass. But if I took you right now, just as you are, you'd die. You couldn't stand the exposure. You don't have the right kind of life."

There was again no answer. The tadpole's tail was scarcely waving at all.

"The vital question," the frog continued, "is whether you're willing to follow the evidence where it leads. You'll not be given more evidence until you use the evidence you have."

Bubu said something that sounded like "Humph." Again there was silence.

The frog stretched his legs uneasily. "It's so stuffy down here," he said. "I have to go up for a gulp of air more frequently these days. So if you'll excuse me . . . ."

Several minutes passed before Bubu moved. The wiggles of his tail had ceased. Perhaps weighty problems occupying his mind accounted for the slowness of his movements. He might have been thinking of the brilliant remarks he could have made had he thought of them in time.

His actual thoughts will never be known, for in his preoccupation he hadn't noticed the swiftly moving black shadow inches behind him.

The duck's bill churned violently downward. Immense jaws clamped upon Bubu's tail, while his body tugged helplessly in the water. He felt himself jerked powerfully upwards. Upwards, and oh unnameable dread, through the surface and into the Great Beyond.

Terrible light and suffering nothingness surrounded him for a brief second. Sounds of unbelievable intensity battered his tortured hearing apparatus. Then, with a swift toss of the duck's head, came hot darkness.

"Another Life" adapted from "Metamorphosis" by John White, *HIS Magazine*, December, 1963, pp. 1–3

Openness

A student, wringing his hands and looking distraught, said to me, "I have a roommate. And I want to witness to him. But I keep wondering when the right time is. I mean, *when* should I *do it* to him? At what moment must I really tell him? How will I know when the exact time is to finally do it?" By the time he had finished his question, he had me feeling as uptight and intense as he was. And I could not help but sympathize with whomever the recipient of this talk would be. That kind of anxiety would scare a person to death!

It is far more winsome to toss out a few casual comments about your relationship to God or about your Bible study. There is something very appealing about openness. Say, "Hey, I'd like you to meet a friend who's in this fantastic Bible study I'm in," or even, "We had an interesting study this week on how Jesus related to women. He sure was ahead of the culture of his day in his attitude toward women." And then see what happens.

We should talk the same way to non-Christians as we do to Christians. In most instances we should be able to tell both groups the same stories or experiences or thoughts. This will help us avoid having an us-and-them mentality. We should not assume that our non-Christian friends will not be interested in our spiritual side. We need to invite them into our lives, to share what we share, enjoy what we enjoy. We must not act superior because we know God or have more information. Rather, we must be, as someone has said, "one beggar sharing with another beggar where to find bread."

Out of the Saltshaker by Rebecca M. Pippert, p. 130

REFLECTIONS

I Stand by the Door

"I stand by the door," he wrote.
"I neither go too far in, nor stay too far out.
The door is the most important door in the
world—
It is the door through which men walk when they
find God. . . .
Men die outside that door, as starving beggars die
On cold nights, in cruel cities, in the dead of
winter—
Nothing else matters compared to helping them
find it,
And open it, and walk in, and find Him. . . .
So I stand by the door. . . .

You can go in too deeply and stay in too long,
And forget the people outside the door.
As for me, I shall take my old accustomed place,
Near enough to God to hear Him, and know He is
there,
But not so far from men as not to hear them,
And remember they are there, too.
Where? Outside the door—
Thousands of them, millions of them.
But—more important for me—
One of them, two of them, ten of them,
Whose hands I am intended to put on the latch.
So I shall stand by the door and wait
For those who seek it.
'I had rather be a door-keeper. . . .'
So I stand by the door."

Sam Shoemaker, Episcopal rector and evangelist

Become a Fisherman

The areas of common interest do not have to be
religious. If your neighbor is a fisherman, become
a fisherman. If he's in the newspaper business, let
him teach you about the newspaper business. I
had the joy of influencing a friend to Christ by
doing just that. He was an executive with the
Dallas Morning News. I asked if he would mind
giving me a tour of the entire operation. I asked
every imaginable question. I was fascinated by all
I saw. We spent one whole day together. I took an
interest in his world. I became a newspaper man.
Shortly thereafter he took an interest in my
world, and became a Christian. A day in the oil
fields with an oil company president produced the
same results. I became an oil man, he became a
Christian. With two of my neighbors, I became a
tennis player, and they became Christians.

Life-Style Evangelism by Joseph C. Aldrich, p. 70

Music of the Gospel

What is the music of the gospel? The *music* of the gospel is the beauty of the indwelling Christ as lived out in the everyday relationships of life. The *gospel* is the good news that Jesus Christ has solved the problem of man's sin and offers him the potential of an exchanged life, a life in which the resources of God Himself are available for his transformation. And as the gospel is translated into music, it makes redemptive relationships possible. When the world observes husbands loving their wives, and wives supporting and caring for their husbands and families, they have seen a miracle; they have heard the music. It is miraculous music for which many of them are longing.

Life-Style Evangelism by Joseph C. Aldrich, p. 20

Caring

A non-Christian girl began going to a church for counseling. She was impressed most, she said later, by the way two of the associate pastors talked to their wives on the telephone, not by the direct help she received. The genuine caring and affection she heard convinced her of the gospel's truth.

I can be certain of two things about every person I meet: God loves him, and he has a need. Personal communication means helping each person take the next step toward Christ or in Christ.

Good News Is for Sharing by Leighton Ford, p. 105

FOUR

REFRAMING QUESTIONS

Even the most energetic among us will not always find witnessing easy. We make contacts, develop friendships, create openings, and then, when we try to witness, we find ourselves stumbling over words and stuttering feeble answers to unexpected questions. Has the Holy Spirit deserted us? No. But even those who have the Spirit's power need to study and practice what to say.

One of the first things we must recognize is that periods of serious discussion with friends will not always be positive. Non-Christians often have negative feelings about the church and stereotyped images of Christ. Since the range of potential questions is so broad—positive and negative, church-centered and Christ-centered—even well-equipped witnesses cannot formulate great answers to all possible subjects beforehand. But working through a short list of typical responses, pro and con, increases our confidence and ability to witness effectively.

Of course, learning the right answers isn't enough. As Rebecca Pippert observes, "The way we communicate is as important as what we communicate. . . . Our attitude and style communicate content just as do our words" (*Out of the Saltshaker*, p. 128).

What attitude should we adopt? Two giant, New Testament apostles give us some guidance. Rough-shod Peter challenges us to answer with "gentleness and respect" (1 Pet. 3:15). Paul, the theologian, counts our demeanor more significant than exactitude and clever words: "Let your conversation be always full of grace, seasoned with salt, so that you may know how to answer everyone" (Col. 4:6). Winsome witnesses, sharing their faith naturally, will never sacrifice friendship for the sake of winning an argument or shaming the indiscreet.

Search for Meaning

In his classic book Man's Search for Meaning, *Viktor E. Frankl uses his three years in a German concentration camp to illustrate that people have an irresistible urge to find purpose and meaning in life. His vivid pictures reveal that even when they were fighting over food or facing immediate extinction in the ovens, these prisoners had their minds on deeper matters. They had an unquenchable desire to hear a legitimate explanation for their unjust treatment, their senseless suffering. Frankl describes some of his attempts to provide that meaning to his fellow sufferers—and admits that, because he often lacked "inner strength," he passed up many opportunities to talk about God.*

Frankl's book reminds us that all people— including the non-Christians we interact with— have a strong "will to meaning." If we don't want to miss opportunities to witness, we must be prepared for serious discussion with our friends. We need to be able to handle their questions in a way that's appropriate and helpful. Working with people's minds, Frankl might say, is essential—the one need that is never snuffed out.

After reading his account, work through the following questions:

▶1. How did Frankl seek to encourage his fellow prisoners in Auschwitz? Do you think he was successful?

▶2. Have you personally learned something of special meaning or value from a time of suffering or grief?

▶3. How might Frankl's story motivate and encourage you in your actual efforts to witness to friends?

Fifteen hundred persons had been traveling by train for several days and nights: there were eighty people in each coach. . . . The carriages were so full that only the top parts of the windows were free to let in the gray of dawn. . . . We did not know whether we were still in Silesia or already in Poland. The engine's whistle had an uncanny sound, like a cry for help sent out in commiseration for the unhappy load. . . . Then the train shunted, obviously nearing a main station. Suddenly a cry broke from the ranks of the anxious passengers, "There is a sign, Ausch- witz!" Everyone's heart missed a beat at that moment. Auschwitz—the very name stood for all that was horrible: gas chambers, crematoriums, massacres. Slowly, almost hesitatingly, the train moved on as if it wanted to spare its passengers the dreadful realization as long as possible: Auschwitz!

With the progressive dawn, the outlines of an immense camp became visible: long stretches of several rows of barbed wire fences; watch towers; search lights; and long columns of ragged human figures, gray in the grayness of dawn, trekking along the straight desolate roads, to what destina- tion we did not know. There were isolated shouts and whistles of command. We did not know their meaning. My imagination led me to see gallows with people dangling on them. I was horrified, but this was just as well, because step by step we had to become accustomed to a terrible and immense horror. . . .

Most of the prisoners were given a uniform of rags which would have made a scarecrow elegant by comparison. Between the huts in the camp lay pure filth, . . . and it was a favorite practice to assign a new arrival the job of cleaning the latrines and removing the sewage. If, as usually happened, some of the excrement splashed into his face during its transport over bumpy fields, any sign of disgust by the prisoner or any attempt to wipe off the filth would only be punished with a blow from a [guard]. . . .

Beatings occurred on the slightest provocation, sometimes for no reason at all. For example, bread was rationed out at our work site and we had to line up for it. Once, the man behind me stood off a little to one side and that lack of symmetry displeased the SS guard. I did not know what was going on in the line behind me, nor in the mind of the SS guard, but suddenly I received two sharp blows on my head. Only then did I spot the guard at my side who was using his stick. At such a moment it is not the physical pain which hurts the most (and this applies to adults as much as to punished children); it is the mental agony caused by the injustice, the unreasonableness of it all. . . .

The most painful part of beatings is the insult which they imply. At one time we had to carry some long, heavy girders over icy tracks. If one man slipped, he endangered not only himself but all the others who carried the same girder. An old friend of mine had a congenitally dislocated hip. He was glad to be capable of working in spite of it, since the physically disabled were almost certainly sent to death when a selection took place. He limped over the track with an especially heavy girder, and seemed about to fall and drag the others with him. As yet, I was not carrying a girder so I jumped to his assistance without stopping to think. I was immediately hit on the back, rudely reprimanded and ordered to return to my place. A few minutes previously the same guard who struck me had told us deprecatingly that we "pigs" lacked the spirit of comradeship.

Another time, in a forest, with the temperature at two degrees fahrenheit, we began to dig up the topsoil, which was frozen hard, in order to lay water pipes. By then I had grown rather weak physically. Along came a foreman with chubby rosy cheeks. His face definitely reminded me of a pig's head. I noticed that he wore lovely warm gloves in that bitter cold. For a time he watched me silently. I felt that trouble was brewing, for in front of me lay the mound of earth which showed exactly how much I had dug.

Then he began: "You pig, I have been watching you the whole time! I'll teach you to work, yet! Wait till you dig dirt with your teeth—you'll die like an animal! In two days I'll finish you off! You've never done a stroke of work in your life. What were you, swine? A businessman?"

I was past caring. But I had to take his threat of killing me seriously, so I straightened up and looked him directly in the eye. "I was a doctor—a specialist."

"What? A doctor? I bet you got a lot of money out of people."

"As it happens, I did most of my work for no money at all, in clinics for the poor." But, now, I had said too much. He threw himself on me and knocked me down, shouting like a madman. . . .

I want to show with this apparently trivial story that there are moments when indignation can rouse even a seemingly hardened prisoner—indignation not about cruelty or pain, but about the insult connected with it. That time blood rushed to my head because I had to listen to a man judge my life who had so little idea of it. . . .

[One night as we sat huddled in our hut] I spoke of the many opportunities of giving life a meaning. I told my comrades (who lay motionless, although occasionally a sigh could be heard) that human life, under any circumstances, never ceases to have meaning, and that this infinite meaning of life includes suffering and dying, privation and death. I asked the poor creatures who listened to me attentively in the darkness of the hut to face up to the seriousness of our position. They must not lose hope but should keep their courage in the certainty that the hopelessness of our struggle did not detract from its dignity and its meaning. I said that someone looks down on each of us in difficult hours—a friend, a wife, somebody alive or dead, or God—and he would not expect us to disappoint him. He would hope to find us suffering proudly—not miserably—knowing how to die.

And finally I spoke of our sacrifice, which had meaning in every case. It was in the nature of this sacrifice that it should appear to be pointless in the normal world, the world of material success.

But in reality our sacrifice did have a meaning. Those of us who had religious faith, I said frankly, could understand without difficulty. I told them of a comrade who on his arrival in camp had tried to make a pact with heaven that his suffering and death should save the human being he loved from a painful end. For this man, suffering and death were meaningful; his was a sacrifice of the deepest significance. He did not want to die for nothing. None of us wanted that.

The purpose of my words was to find a full meaning in our life, then and there, in that hut and in that practically hopeless situation. I saw that my efforts had been successful. When the electric bulb flared up again, I saw the miserable figures of my friends limping toward me to thank me with tears in their eyes. But I have to confess that only too rarely had I the inner strength to make contact with my companions in suffering and that I must have missed many opportunities for doing so.

Man's Search for Meaning by Viktor E. Frankl, pp. 12–13, 31–32, 35–39, 131–133

Bible Study: 1 Peter 3:15–16

Peter stresses that upright behavior and a reasoned statement of faith go together. Non-Christians typically respond first to a distinctive life-style, but when they raise sincere questions, they rightly expect a coherent answer. Recall the most recent or memorable occasion when someone asked you to explain your faith. What was the question, and what was your answer? In answering did you meet Peter's criterion of "gentleness and respect"?

Always be prepared to give an answer to everyone who asks you to give the reason for the hope that you have. But do this with gentleness and respect, keeping a clear conscience, so that those who speak maliciously against your good behavior in Christ may be ashamed of their slander.

1 Peter 3:15–16

Redefining the Issues

Carl Schroeder demonstrates that the skill of reframing is vital for witness. It's a skill Paul used in his encounter with the Philippian jailer (Acts 16:25–40). In response to the jailer's fearful cry, "What must I do to save my skin?" Paul directed him to eternal salvation.

If we have the ability to redefine the issues in this way, we will catch statements or questions that suggest a desire for change. Reworking our friends' inquiries or remarks keeps us sensitive and prevents us from trying to manipulate them. Particularly in a secular world, where misunderstanding occurs easily because we lack a common ground for communicating, reframing is vital.

Can you improve on the reframing in the illustrations below?

▶1. Statement: "I just can't go on this way."
Reframed: "Do you mean that you are unhappy with your life as it is now and feel the need to make some basic changes?"
(The likely response will be positive, enabling further exploration of the person's eagerness for a life change, including conversion.)

▶2. Statement: "I don't know where we go from here."
Reframed: "Are you wondering what we might do next to help you get some changes under way?"

▶3. Statement: "I'd like to go back to church, but something always gets in the way."
Reframed: "Do you mean that you feel unable to take the step of coming back to the church and to Christ by yourself—that your own strength is just not enough?"

▶4. Statement: "I know that you have happiness and peace. I wish I could have that in my life. I just can't find it."
Reframed: "Do you mean that if you were able to make the changes in your life that I have made in mine, you might find the kind of happiness that you see in me?"

▶5. Statement: "Sometimes I wish I could live parts of my life over again, but I guess it's too late for that now."
Reframed: "Are you saying that you feel bad about some of your past behaviors and wish that you could change them now, but feel that it's too late to change?"

The skill of reframing keeps the persons we are trying to reach in charge of the conversation. They do not feel manipulated if they sense that they themselves have made the moves leading to their own conversion. Thus, phrases like "Do you mean . . . . ?" and "Are you saying . . . . ?" are crucial because they often aim the issues in a more helpful direction. In addition, reframing offers persons the opportunity to affirm what they really mean, not necessarily what we want them to say.

Crises

Respond to these crisis situations. Use your personal experience where applicable.

▶ 1. "I just discovered my son is on drugs. Where can I get help?"

▶ 2. "I really don't have much to live for since my husband died."

▶ 3. "Our children don't seem to care for us at all. They never visit us."

▶ 4. "I found out this morning that my little brother was driving drunk last night and had a wreck. He's in the hospital and has hurt two other people pretty bad. I don't know what to do or what to say to him."

Prepare some guidelines for dealing with crises. Remember that people are often more reflective than usual when they are dealing with a death in the family, an accident, an illness, or a lost job. So times of emotional and physical stress provide a special opportunity for witness.

At such times, our friends are usually open and sometimes ready to consider a radically new life direction (though often the change does not occur until after the immediate emergency is over). What guidelines would you recommend for witnessing during a crisis?

▶ 1.

▶ 2.

▶ 3.

As Western society becomes . . . increasingly pagan . . . how are we to make the Gospel meaningful? . . . . We must appreciate the outlook and problems of those we are trying to reach. Otherwise we are in very real danger of talking at cross purposes. . . . So we need not be surprised if when we speak of man's guilt, (our hearers) will assume that we mean psychological guilt rather than moral guilt before God, which is what the Bible speaks of.

The Gospel in a Pagan Society by
Kenneth F. W. Prior,
pp. 8, 39, 57

REFLECTIONS

Five Challenges

How can we respond appropriately to these situations in which the credibility of Christian truth is being attacked? Remember the biblical guidelines in 1 Peter 3:15–16 and Colossians 4:6. Drawing the person out may reveal deeper concerns; hearing them is more important than giving a technically correct answer.

▶1. *"How Do You Know?"* A friend to whom you have witnessed by using the Bible to explain who Jesus is, suddenly bursts out, "But what makes you think that stuff is really true? There are lots of other so-called holy books. Why is this one any different from the Koran or that Mormon book? It could all be a big fairy tale."

▶2. *"As Calloused as Heathens."* You have been trying to show a friend that Christians are admonished to love all people, including their enemies. The friend has listened "with a knowing smile," pointing out instances in which so-called Christians have been just as calloused to others' problems as heathens are. "Remember that self-righteous woman in Florida several years ago who tried to eliminate all homosexuals from the public school teaching staffs? Christians become just as hostile as anyone when they don't like somebody," your friend concludes.

▶3. *"It's as Bogus as Advertising."* John sat up late one night and watched a "Christian" television program. He saw a man who was recently "born again" claiming that because of his new life-style, his business was picking up after months of stagnation, his marriage was pulling together after several rocky years, and his children were becoming more responsible and obedient.

John was incredulous and incensed by the claims. As he sat and watched he thought of Ken, a guy at the office who made frequent attempts to discuss the Christian faith with his coworkers.

The next day John approached Ken. He wanted to know how Ken could be part of a movement that sounds like the old-fashioned "cure-all" and is really a blatant rip-off based on false promises.

▶4. *"Jesus and Old Age Homes."* The college student was unimpressed with Jesus' relevance for today. "He may have been a great leader, but that was another country and another century. What did he accomplish that is of any value now? He never had a teenage son on drugs. He never was forsaken to rot in an old age home. He never worked on an assembly line doing a meaningless job."

▶5. *"Santa Claus and Other Myths."* "Science has ruled out the possibility of belief in a personal God. We no longer require the idea of God to explain the world. Physics and geology offer everything we need without God. Belief in a God who maintains the universe is a fable that we should cast aside—just as we have ridded ourselves of astrology, Santa Claus, and other myths."

Objections to Church

Below are typical responses to church life. How would you recommend they be reframed so that the discussion can move forward fruitfully rather than turn into a pointless confrontation?

▶1. "Church was something I needed once. But relatively speaking, I'm now a more mature person, a whole person. I don't feel the need for the church today—though I grant there may be children and certain adults who still find that institution important to their stability."

▶2. "I live for the weekends. That's my busy time—camping, celebrating with friends, sports. There's always something going on, and I find it refreshing. When the church offers something better, I'll consider attending."

▶3. "If we all serve one God, I don't understand why there are so many churches. Something must be wrong somewhere or we wouldn't have such disharmony. When the churches unite and stop fighting each other, I'll start taking them more seriously."

▶4. "The people with the inside track in most churches are the folks with good names, money, or business connections. They're the big shots. I want to be accepted for myself—not some artificial standards. So I guess the church has no place for me."

Bad Timing

"In my early Christian life, when I first began witnessing to my friends, the great hurdle was always getting started. I never seemed to know what to say. I began keeping a page of 'openers' in a notebook. These are questions I would ask to get into the subject. They included: "Was there ever a time in your life when you seriously considered becoming a Christian?" "What did you think of the sermon?" "Are you interested in spiritual things?"

Such questions can help. But they often back-fired on me. I could never seem to get the timing right. I would 'casually' throw these questions out in the midst of an otherwise normal conversation. At that point everything became abnormal. My quarry would tense up—and become almost as tense as I was. Then, electrically, I would go into my presentation. This approach was just as alien as the opening question. It consisted of heavy offers of eternal life and vague references to happiness now. Where there is incongruence between our words and the situation, that's about all we have to offer. What we represent is not substantially any different from what the receiver already has. Even eternal life is not particularly attractive to him. He's already ambivalent about the life he does have—both hating and loving it, but not loving it enough to want to go on forever.

Evangelism as a Lifestyle by Jim Peterson, pp. 79–80

REFLECTIONS

Turning the Tables

We can learn to ask good questions. Too often we allow ourselves to be put on the defensive. The dynamics are greatly changed when we turn the tables and begin to direct the conversation by asking questions. I remember a skeptical student who said, "I could never be a Christian. My commitment to scholarship makes any consideration of Christianity impossible. It's irrational, and the evidence supporting it is totally insufficient."

I answered, "I'm so glad you care so much about truth and that you really want evidence to support your beliefs. You say the evidence for Christianity is terribly insufficient. What was your conclusion after carefully investigating the primary biblical documents?"

"Ah, well, you mean the Bible?" he asked.

"Of course," I said. "The New Testament accounts of Jesus, for example. Where did you find them lacking?"

"Oh, well, look, I remember Mother reading me those stories when I was ten," he replied.

"Hmm, but what was your conclusion?" I continued and as a result discovered he had never investigated the Scriptures critically as an adult. This is all too often the case. But we can arouse curiosity in others to investigate the claims of the gospel when we help them see their information and understanding about Christianity is lacking.

Out of the Saltshaker by Rebecca M. Pippert, p. 132

A Swim to Hawaii

The late Paul Little used an analogy that could go like this:

Tom: Well, I'm not perfect, but I think I'm as good as a lot of other people, and better than some.

Jim: That may be true, but put it like this. Suppose we all lined up on the West Coast to swim to Hawaii. One person might only get 25 yards from the beach. Someone else might make 100 yards. If you're a good swimmer, you might make five miles. But who's going to make it to Hawaii?

Tom: Nobody.

Jim: In the same way, I may be better than somebody else, but I still come short as far as God is concerned.

Good News Is for Sharing by Leighton Ford, p. 174

FIVE

LISTENING

Good friends listen to each other. By listening we reach through to what Paul Tournier calls another's person—to the frightened person behind the good front, to the generous person behind a boring exterior, to the beautiful person behind a homely face. A friendship of trust and support is built on good listening.

Many of us wrongly assume that while speaking takes practice, listening comes naturally. In fact, listening is a complicated enterprise that demands our whole person—at least if we are to hear the meaning behind words, interpret posture and tone of voice, and get beyond facts to feelings. The singer John Lennon legitimately complained about most of us: "Your voice is like Musak to my ears." We all can and should learn when to keep silent. We all can and should improve our listening skills.

Good listening is an essential part of friendship witnessing. As Christians we should make it our aim to listen through the biblical filters of creation, fall, and redemption. In so doing, we will come to see others and know others as God has created them—as unique, gifted individuals. We will be able to respond to their brokenness. And we'll listen carefully for signs of hope and redemption.

Skilled listeners connect with the soul, not merely with the will or the intellect. They listen as willingly to expressions of loneliness or joy as to cries of guilt. It's very likely that understanding and rehearsing the witnessing process will multiply our witness tenfold.

Bible Study

The Old Testament is full of poignant cries from God, reprimanding his people for not listening to him (see, for example, Jer. 11:8–10). And in the New Testament that emphasis on listening continues: Jesus commends Mary for sitting at his feet and listening while her sister Martha struggles in the kitchen.

Obviously, listening to God should be our first priority. Yet we need to listen to others as well. Jesus himself did—often. Recall a few of the many times that Christ paused in an incredibly busy ministry to listen—and respond—to people around him.

Conclude by reflecting briefly on these wise words:

He who answers before listening—that is his folly and his shame.

Proverbs 18:13

Everyone should be quick to listen, slow to speak and slow to become angry . . . ."

James 1:19

Active Listening

Practice using silent gestures of approval, such as smiling and nodding your head "yes." Be liberal with affirming words: "tell me more" or "keep coming" or "I appreciate knowing that" or "do you mean. . . ?" or "did I hear correctly?" or "you did, huh?" or "I see" or "hmmmm" or "interesting" or "oh" or "really?"

Active listening involves feedback—the listener must repeat some of the talker's thoughts and feelings without changing meaning or adding anything new. Keep quiet about your opinions until your friend asks for them or until you have more information; the trust that comes from patience will make your friendship stronger.

The following brief example of active listening is adapted from *Stop, Love, and Listen*, produced by Christian Reformed Home Missions. Notice how active listening encourages talkers to share important personal information and prompts them to tell more because of the mutual bond that develops.

Summary
1. Talker describes events and feelings.
2. Listener restates those events and feelings.

Result
1. Talker appreciates being understood and accepted.
2. Listener increases in understanding of talker.

TALKER	**LISTENER**

TALKER

1. Wow! It seems like prices just keep going up. And up and up and up!

3. Yeah. Just when I thought I had some money ahead, I'm clobbered with a rent hike.

5. Well, I'm trying to save up for a vacation, but—hey! If things don't change, I'll be stuck in this miserable place forever!

7. Oh, it isn't everything, but my job isn't going well. There's stress there.

9. Uh-huh. So, here I am with a job I don't like, no money, car repairs, and no way to get away from it all. And that's not all!

11. Well, my brother is mad at me. We've always gotten along great until lately.

13. Sure! And it's his own stupid fault. Ever since he got mixed up with religion, he's been on the kooky side. And he wants me to go to church with him. That's a laugh!

15. No way! I wouldn't go inside a church for all the money in Miami. Never met a church person who wasn't a hypocrite.

17. None of 'em!

19. They're always leaning on you for money. That's what it's all about—taking your money. Bleed you dry. It's going to happen to him. I keep telling him, but he doesn't listen to me.

21. Yeah. I want for people to listen to me.

23. Why can't he? You do. You let me talk. You understand what I'm saying. I can trust you.

25. I keep telling him, "You don't know what they're trying to do to you."

27. I don't want him ripped off. He won't listen. He just keeps inviting me to go too.

29. Like I said, I wouldn't go near one of those places.

31. Uh, yeah—you've got it . . . Oh boy, now I see something else. Like you just said, I'm telling him, but he's been there.

33. So maybe I don't know what I'm talking about.

LISTENER

2. Like they'll go out of sight!

4. It's hit you pretty hard.

6. You sound very discouraged—maybe about several things.

8. And that stress slops over into other parts of life.

10. I don't know if there's any way I can help, but if you want to talk about it some more, I'm sure willing to listen.

12. That must really hurt!

14. Not your style right now.

16. As far as you're concerned, you can't trust any of them.

18. Not even one.

20. You want him to listen to you, but he doesn't, so it frustrates you.

22. That's really important.

24. Thanks.

26. You want to warn him.

28. Which you don't do.

30. So you keep telling him what they're up to, and he keeps inviting you to come see for yourself.

32. So . . . ?

34. Are you thinking it might be time to find out for yourself?

Listening Through Biblical Filters

When we listen to our friends, it's important that we listen for more than spiritual talk *about* Jesus and salvation; we listen for signs of creation, fall, and redemption behind their ordinary words. Our listening penetrates to the spiritual level.

How do we know if we're actually listening through the biblical filters of creation, fall, and redemption? The following questions can serve as guidelines for listeners:

▶1. *Creation:* What signs do I see that this person is a unique, gifted individual, created by God?

▶2. *Fall:* Where in this person's language do I hear signs of weakness, failure, hurt, need?

▶3. *Redemption:* What evidence do I hear of healing, victory, reconciliation, freedom, restoration?

A Step Further

Carefully read the following story from A Step Further *by Joni Eareckson, a woman who has been paralyzed from the neck down since a diving accident when she was seventeen. As you read the story, practice listening with your biblical filters in place. How do Joni's comments reflect creation, the fall, and (especially) redemption?*

Have you ever noticed how the things in life that have the greatest potential for good also have an unusual potential for bad? Take fire, for instance, one of man's greatest discoveries. The same flame that cooks a steak can also ruin acres of precious forest within a matter of minutes—or burn down a barn. And what about sex? It, too, can be very good and very bad. Although God meant it to bind husbands and wives together, give them pleasure, and bring them children, its misuse brings guilt, heartache, and tears.

So it is with suffering. While it is God's choicest tool to mold our character, it also has the tendency to breed self-centeredness. I've wasted hours pitying myself and getting all wrapped up in imagining that my broken neck was God's way of getting even with me for my sins, when in reality He was far from being "out to get me."

Our God is a wonderful God. Just one good look at the miracle of childbirth, the beauty of nature, or the complexity of the solar system can tell us that. These awesome wonders give us a glimpse of how powerful, creative, and wise He is. But God has other qualities, too, virtues men would never see if suffering and sin didn't give them a chance to show themselves.

Take His kindness, for instance. Would we really appreciate the good health He gives us if none of us were ever sick? Would God's forgiveness ever grip us if He never let us feel the piercing guilt of our sins? And what about His compassion in answering our prayers? How would we learn of it if we never had any needs to pray about? You see, the problems we face highlight the mercies of our God.

But not only that—our problems provide a showcase for the good qualities that people have too. Though bad in themselves, our problems allow people to show concern and other kindnesses to one another. . . . Suffering sets the stage on which good qualities can perform. If we never had to face fear, we would know nothing about courage. If we never had to weep, we would not know what it was like to have a friend wipe tears from our eyes.

But what does all of this have to do with God? When I say that suffering is able to bring out the best in us, am I singing some sort of hymn to human goodness? Not at all! By praising human goodness I'm actually praising God's goodness. For, you see, God is the author of every good and noble thing in the world (James 1:17). All of the love, kindness, sharing, and forgiveness that one person has ever shown to another comes ultimately from Him. We are made in His image— even those of us who don't acknowledge Him. Of course, that image is marred and tainted by sin. But it's still there, and whenever we do something good . . . we prove it!

excerpts from *A Step Further* by Joni Eareckson

The Ear Is a Muscle

Just as muscles can be strengthened through exercise, the ear's hearing ability can be improved. Here are two simple exercises for increasing the ear's capacity for listening.

1. Sit quietly for two minutes; close your eyes and listen for every possible sound. Afterwards, jot down what you heard. What sounds did listening so intently help you hear for the first time?

2. Select a friend, family member, or classmate (if you are studying this book as part of a group). Tell him or her five facts about yourself (hobbies, places you have visited, names of favorite people, best-liked foods, and so forth). Then see if your partner can recall your list. Keep exchanging lists of five as time permits. Did listening intently and concentrating help you remember?

REFLECTIONS

The Magic Eyes

Lewis Smedes opens his book Forgive and Forget *with his little fable about Fouke and the magic eyes. The fable illustrates our need to listen for the hidden emotions and motives of those to whom we witness.*

In the village of Faken in innermost Friesland there lived a long thin baker named Fouke, a righteous man, with a long thin chin and a long thin nose. Fouke was so upright that he seemed to spray righteousness from his thin lips over everyone who came near him; so the people of Faken preferred to stay away.

Fouke's wife, Hilda, was short and round, her arms were round, her bosom was round, her rump was round. Hilda did not keep people at bay with righteousness; her soft roundness seemed to invite them instead to come close to her in order to share the warm cheer of her open heart.

Hilda respected her righteous husband, and loved him too, as much as he allowed her; but her heart ached for something more from him than his worthy righteousness.

And there, in the bed of her need, lay the seed of sadness.

One morning, having worked since dawn to knead his dough for the ovens, Fouke came home and found a stranger in his bedroom lying on Hilda's round bosom.

Hilda's adultery soon became the talk of the tavern and the scandal of the Faken congregation. Everyone assumed that Fouke would cast Hilda out of his house, so righteous was he. But he surprised everyone by keeping Hilda as his wife, saying he forgave her as the Good Book said he should.

In his heart of hearts, however, Fouke could not forgive Hilda for bringing shame to his name. Whenever he thought about her, his feelings toward her were angry and hard; he despised her as if she were a common whore. When it came right down to it, he hated her for betraying him after he had been so good and so faithful a husband to her.

He only pretended to forgive Hilda so that he could punish her with his righteous mercy.

But Fouke's fakery did not sit well in heaven.

So each time that Fouke would feel his secret hate toward Hilda, an angel came to him and dropped a small pebble, hardly the size of a shirt button, into Fouke's heart. Each time a pebble dropped, Fouke would feel a stab of pain like the pain he felt the moment he came on Hilda feeding her hungry heart from a stranger's larder.

Thus he hated her the more; his hate brought him pain and his pain made him hate.

The pebbles multiplied. And Fouke's heart grew very heavy with the weight of them, so heavy that the top half of his body bent forward so far that he had to strain his neck upward in order to see straight ahead. Weary with hurt, Fouke began to wish he were dead.

The angel who dropped the pebbles into his heart came to Fouke one night and told him how he could be healed of his hurt.

There was one remedy, he said, only one, for the hurt of a wounded heart. Fouke would need the miracle of the magic eyes. He would need eyes that could look back to the beginning of his hurt and see his Hilda, not as a wife who betrayed him, but as a weak woman who needed him. Only a new way of looking at things through the magic eyes could heal the hurt flowing from the wounds of yesterday.

Fouke protested. "Nothing can change the past," he said. "Hilda is guilty, a fact that not even an angel can change."

"Yes, poor hurting man, you are right," the angel said. "You cannot change the past, you can only heal the hurt that comes to you from the past. And you can heal it only with the vision of the magic eyes."

"And how can I get your magic eyes?" pouted Fouke.

"Only ask, desiring as you ask, and they will be given you. And each time you see Hilda through your new eyes, one pebble will be lifted from your aching heart."

Fouke could not ask at once, for he had grown to love his hatred. But the pain of his heart finally drove him to want and to ask for the magic eyes that the angel had promised. So he asked. And the angel gave.

Soon Hilda began to change in front of Fouke's eyes, wonderfully and mysteriously. He began to see her as a needy woman who loved him instead of a wicked woman who betrayed him.

The angel kept his promise; he lifted the pebbles from Fouke's heart, one by one, though it took a long time to take them all away. Fouke gradually felt his heart grow lighter; he began to walk straight again, and somehow his nose and his chin seemed less thin and sharp than before. He invited Hilda to come into his heart again, and she came, and together they began again a journey into their second season of humble joy.

Forgive and Forget: Healing the Hurts We Don't Deserve by Lewis Smedes, pp. xiii-xv

REFLECTIONS

Confidentiality

The more confidential we become in our conversation, the more important it is that we never disclose private information to someone else. Unless our friends believe we will protect confidentiality, we will never learn any deep facts about them.

▶ Must we make this an absolute rule, refusing to tell even our spouses, for example, what we were told in confidence?

▶ If there are exceptions, what kinds?

▶ For what possible reasons could we ever jeopardize friendships for the sake of retaining the right to tell others what our friends tell us?

The Art of Listening

To be a good listener requires interest in the subject under discussion and a desire to retain that information. This is not always easy. You may ask a question and elicit a response which you thought would interest you. But while the person is responding, you tend to start thinking about your answer to what has just been said, or you formulate the next question. As a result you *hear* what was said, but don't remember the *content* of the response. This is usually quite apparent to the one who was doing the talking. You yourself may have experienced that hurt feeling which comes when, after pouring your heart out to someone, you realize that he or she wasn't even listening.

Listening is an art which is learned through practice. Psychiatrists advocate a method called "active listening," in which you paraphrase and condense what the individual has just said and repeat it back to him or her. It is a good exercise, one that I would recommend highly. However, it requires not only listening to words, but also understanding the messages sent by facial expressions, body positions, eye movements, and hand gestures. Listening is also a complete body function on your part, for you too are sending messages. Watch someone who is concentrating on what is being said. He leans forward expectantly, focusing his entire being on the speaker and what he is saying. This should be your posture as an evangelist, because good listening is *agape* in action.

Agape Evangelism—Roots that Reach Out by
Richard G. Korthals, pp. 43–44

Six

TESTIMONIES

A well-equipped witness knows how to tell her story. She can talk easily and naturally about how Jesus has affected her life, changed her outlook, given her hope. She can give a testimony that likely will have a powerful impact on her friends.

Those of us who don't feel able, ready, or prepared to tell our faith-story freely have to work at it, practice it, refine it. Through our testimonies we demonstrate that our faith is alive and genuine. We show that we are personally convinced about the gospel and not just promoting a charade of theoretical answers to life's problems. Certainly our witness must point to the facts of the Bible and to Christ: "For we do not preach ourselves, but Jesus Christ as Lord" (2 Cor. 4:5). But we preach our Lord in *personal* terms: "I have been crucified with Christ and I no longer live, but Christ lives in me."

In friendship witness we want others to believe in Christ, not just know facts about him. For that to happen, we need to share personal experiences that center on Christ. Otherwise Christ will remain only at the hazy edges of our friendships.

When Peter instructs us (1 Pet. 3:15) to "always be prepared to give a reason for the hope that you have," he recognizes that our various spiritual journeys differ radically. The God who fashions each snowflake works with beautiful variety in each person's life. Paul's testimony, told three times in the book of Acts, is a dramatic account of a lightning conversion (Acts 9, 22, 26); Timothy's is a story of gradual spiritual growth (2 Tim. 1:5–6). But both testimonies reveal the solid faith of the men who proclaim them.

Our testimonies should be accounts of God's faithfulness and love—declarations of deeply moving encounters between our Savior and us. The Holy Spirit uses these self-disclosures to bring a personal Redeemer into our circle of friends.

Sample Testimonies

Later in this chapter you will be asked to write your own testimony. To stimulate your thinking, read through the following actual testimonies from a variety of Christians who tell how they have come alive in Christ.

1. "I am 92. I came from a religious family and even attended church off and on throughout my life. But when someone asked me one day whether I knew for sure that I would go to heaven, I couldn't say yes. That very night was my time of turning to the Lord. I prayed to receive Christ. For thirty years I had put off an operation for fear I would die in surgery. Now I am ready for the hospital. I know where I am going if there is trouble."

2. "I was born and raised in a Christian home but never knew the true joys of Christ. I only knew feelings of emptiness and void. I went through thirteen years of life outside of the church, thinking that it was a dying institution. Not until some very bad things happened in my life did I recognize what I was missing and what was causing my emptiness. I went back to church and this time discovered a group of people whose lives had been touched by Christ. I could feel his presence in every service. The witness of these people brought me back to the Lord. My life is now filled with the love and joy of Christ that I want very much to share with others."

3. "I've been retired for a number of years now. I had the advantage of being raised in a Christian family, and I have known the Lord all my life. The church, my pastors, my Christian wife, my friends, and certainly the Holy Spirit have convinced me I am a sinner before God. But Jesus

Every Christian has a personal story to tell. . . . God has called you to be a very specific, very special person, and your story, your life, is a testimony to God's goodness, his grace, his forgiveness. So share who you are with people. Let them know you have struggles, but that Jesus has made a difference.

Out of the Saltshaker by
Rebecca M. Pippert, pp. 162–63

Christ has saved me from my sin and made me a new person. With the guidance of the Holy Spirit, I want to live a life of gratitude to God, to tell others the good news of God's love!"

4. "I was burdened with guilt and my husband's unfaithfulness. Every night I would read my Bible and pray that this wasn't happening to me. But the problem didn't go away. The story came out, and my marriage fell apart. I was so down that one day I concluded, 'There is no God—he has not heard my prayers.' I spent that night in total darkness of spirit. But when I awoke the next morning, the sun was shining, and I had a peace and joy in my heart that passed all understanding. What I had wanted and searched for so long had become real—Jesus Christ became my personal Savior. I knew that Jesus had bled and died on the cross for me.

"Later that day I picked up my Bible and started reading. The words had a special meaning for me. I knew that God would give me strength for whatever happened in the future. He cared enough to die for me; I will live for him with his guidance. He guided me through a divorce, and he was head of my household as I raised two young children. He continues to bless me with unexpected joy. Jesus is the peace and joy of my life."

5. "I grew most in my faith during crisis. I was fresh out of college and had loads of ambition. I wanted to make millions in business with my father—but it didn't quite work out that way. Dad and I suffered from low prices and rising costs.

We really had to struggle to make it. Coming from the happy-go-lucky life-style of college into the pressure cooker of a tough business was difficult for me. Finally I realized I couldn't make the transition myself. I began to pray about my problem (I hadn't done that in years). And my faith grew in the simple act of praying. I was amazed. I had seen people who had tremendous amounts of faith in God, but I didn't know how they developed that faith until I started praying. I mean it when I say I am very thankful that I know Jesus Christ is my Savior."

6. "When my son lost his life in World War II, I wondered how God could do such a terrible thing to me. I was full of grief and angry at God. I left the church and for twenty years drifted away from God. One day a neighbor invited me to join her Bible-study group. From then on, like a magnet, I was drawn back to God. The Holy Spirit was ever present, but it took the kind Christian neighbor to help me realize how wrong my life was. Now I am a professing member of the church and have found new meaning in life."

7. "Bedridden and crippled with arthritis, I saw only the dark side of life. When Larry came the first time, I didn't know if I cared to visit or not. In fact, when I heard that he had come to talk about Jesus, I was upset. But Larry is a kind person. Even though I often rebuffed him, he came back again and again, just to share some of the news of the day and something of the Good News too. Then God worked in me. It was a joy to be baptized in the name of the Father, Son, and Holy Ghost. Life is different now."

Thought Question

A personal testimony, according to this chapter, is a good way of putting our witness into words. Sometimes we run into difficulties with our testimonies. We find that (whether we intend them to or not) our stories turn our friends' attention to us instead of to Christ. Or, especially if we have a dramatic story to tell, we give our friends the impression that our experience is normative and that anything else falls short. But in spite of these limitations, preparing a testimony is essential for every well-equipped witness; it is a task we cannot choose to ignore.

▶Do you have any objections to that conclusion? If so, work through your reservations and difficulties. Talk about them with friends (or, if you are in a group study with members of your group).

Preparing a Testimony

Take fifteen minutes or so to prepare a brief personal testimony that you could use in friendship witness. The testimony should be short enough to present in less than two minutes. It could either focus on your conversion or be an elaboration on opening lines such as these:

1. I found peace of mind when...
2. Success didn't answer my deepest needs so...
3. I didn't know real love until I experienced Christ's love for me...
4. My life right now shows what Christ can do. I used to be...
5. I grew most in my faith during a crisis that...
6. People (or groups) that have helped me the most are...
7. When we moved for the third time in six years...
8. My church life and religious faith seemed to take on new and deeper meaning when...
9. I discovered how real Jesus is to me when...
10. I used to take my Christian faith for granted, but then...
11. My Christian faith never used to give me much joy, but now...

Be sure to make your testimony friendly and conversational (thinking of a specific person as you write can be helpful). Also remember that avoiding cliches and theological jargon is crucial when communicating to those untrained in the Bible or religious traditions.

If you are writing your testimony in a group setting, you may find time limitations and distractions frustrating. Relax! You can begin your testimony now and finish it later at home. Today you'll be invited to read what you've written so far. Seek advice on ways to improve its precision and clarity.

If you have not discovered much to write about, consider keeping a journal in which you can jot down obvious evidences of God in your life as they occur. Recording these events will help you remember them and will enable you to tell your friends about them.

Once your testimony is completed to your satisfaction, practice until you can present it smoothly and effectively. Obviously you don't want your story to sound canned and rehearsed— and you will certainly want to adapt it to your listener and the occasion. But unless you're confident of what to say, you may end up saying nothing at all.

REFLECTIONS

Preparing a Spiritual Autobiography

Once you've completed your personal testimony, you should also begin working on a somewhat longer "spiritual autobiography"—a record of those life experiences in which your relationship to Christ became more clearly defined and focused.

Most likely you won't be reciting your spiritual autobiography to someone you're witnessing to (though parts of it may be appropriate). The purpose of writing your spiritual autobiography is to help you shape your own understanding of God's work in your life, to jog your memory and remind you of God's faithfulness.

The length of your spiritual story is entirely up to you. As a rough guideline, prsonal testimonies usually run a few paragraphs; spiritual autobiographies may run several pages or more. You needn't finish the autobiography this week, but do plan to complete it soon. You'll find it a challenging but rewarding experience.

Where do you begin? One approach is simply to organize your material chronologically. Reach as far back into your childhood as may be relevant, simply selecting and describing those events that positively or negatively shaped your relationship to Christ.

Or, if you prefer, organize your material thematically. First tell about your life before you accepted Christ as Savior and Lord. Then explain when and how you became more secure in your relationship with him. Finally, tell what your life has been like since you turned it over to Christ.

For some people, of course, the chronological approach and the thematic approach are identical. They have followed a straight path from a life of sin to faith to their walk as believers.

Whatever method of organization you use, please consider these additional suggestions:

1. Use personal language (I, me, my, etc.). Write as though you're talking to someone. Try to avoid words that you wouldn't normally use or that have lost their punch through overuse (wonderful, glorious, fantastic, terrific, etc.).

2. Be specific. Use concrete examples without becoming tedious. You may want to begin by trying to recall every episode that shaped your relationship to Christ. But then eliminate some that may be unduly repetitious. Avoid giving a travelogue focused on externals. Paul tells us about his travels to Damascus, but he doesn't describe the view of Jerusalem as he rode off into the sunset and he doesn't tell us about his personal aches and pains.

3. Never condemn. Be candid, tough, and realistic without judging people harshly (not "my father was domineering and never showed me any love" but "I often felt my father didn't love me and dominated me, but I now realize I did little to help the relationship along."). Being unduly negative about churches or individuals or groups is simply not helpful to yourself or others.

My Mother's Tears

This memorable story recalls an unforgettable moment in author James C. Schaap's life. Obviously God was at work through Schaap's parents, teaching life-long lessons about forgiveness, character, and virtue.

The story demonstrates the kind of experiences that should be included in one's spiritual auto-biography. After you read the story, think about similar incidents from your own childhood, incidents that gave you penetrating insights into yourself or helped you understand life in general.

The Red Owl store had only one checkout aisle, a broad, Formica-topped counter the size of a town flag, with a cash register at the close end, where the checker stood making polite conversation while punching in the prices and jerking back the lever to register the sale.

"Nice tomatoes today, John."

"Aren't they, though?"

Tick, tick—shiick, shiick.

Just behind the counter, the candy rack stood like a buffet, stocked with candy bars, bubble gum, Life Savers, baseball cards, and penny candy wrapped in cellophane. Up above, a flat, wire dispenser advertising Kools held a couple dozen brands of cigarettes, in a system of separate chutes that emptied slowly when the clerk grabbed the bottom pack.

We found stealing cigarettes to be no difficult task. As long as someone was taking her sugar and milk and Cheerios out of her cart and putting them up on the counter, we were free to roam behind the checker. I don't remember the first time I pocketed a pack myself—probably because the job seemed so easy. At first, one pack was plenty for an afternoon of smoking for us, but soon stealing became something of a game. Once, my friend made it out with three packs of Kents, stuffing them down beneath his belt and into his underwear before flipping a dime up on the counter for two packs of baseball cards. What's more, he got Henry Aaron in the process.

But we got caught. I will never forget that night in my bedroom. I'll never forget the way my own father cried as he looked away from me and out the little circular window to the south. I was twelve, I think, and it was summer—the last week in June. I had pretended to be asleep because I knew that the jig was up and all of us were going to catch it; but my parents had snapped on all the lights and marched upstairs and stood there at the foot of my bed. And it all came out in tears.

Three times in two weeks my mother cried for me. That was the first time. My father sat on my bed and talked slowly, trying to wrench out every last piece of information. But my mother didn't say much at all. She couldn't. She was choked up with tears. I was the baby, the only boy. She never guessed I could be stealing, and smoking, cigarettes. She cried out of sheer disappointment, I think. I say that because I'm a parent myself now, and I think I know what I'd feel if my son or daughter did what I did as a boy.

Even then I understood that it was her disappointment that brought those tears. Neither my father nor my mother hit me that night. They didn't have to. I saw both of them cry. I never forgot that, and I never will.

My father sentenced me to two weeks of white-picket-fence painting in the backyard. In addition, I had to pay back John, the Red Owl storekeeper. I went to the store with a pile of fifty-cent pieces, my father right there at my side, pushing me forward, forcing me to tell the man what I'd done. The Red Owl is a shoe store now, and that John isn't selling groceries. But even today I cannot see him without feeling guilt.

For two weeks I saw nothing at all of my friends. For two weeks our family ate around the kitchen table and talked so guardedly that it seemed our words were precious china.

When my sentence was over, we boys got back together. We were raising fantail pigeons in a coop out behind the garage where we used to smoke. We needed straw for bedding, so one day we tied a wagon to the back of one of our bikes and rode up to an old barn at the edge of town. We asked the guy who owned the place if we could have a couple of sacks of straw. He said okay, and we pedaled back to the neighborhood, three stuffed gunny sacks jammed into a coaster wagon swinging behind us.

My father was gone, off to work. My mother took one look at the loot and thought we were stealing again. This time she hit me—hard, as I remember, and often. I remember feeling her hand almost lifting me from the gravel as she swatted me, time and time again, half-running across the alley, pushing me along through the evergreens, across the lawn, and into the back door, then right upstairs, constantly thrashing away at my backside in an explosion of emotion that was, once again, full of tears.

I couldn't tell her that this time I wasn't guilty. I tried, but she was incapable of listening. I remember her screaming at me and I remember thinking that nothing I could say could stop the torrent.

That was the second time she cried, and I know now that it wasn't just from disappointment as it had been the first time. This time there was more. Anger laced the disappointment so tightly that her tears flushed from another emotion. Two weeks earlier they'd come in sobs. This time they came in heaves spliced into a tantrum of fury. That her son could turn right around and do it again after the sheer pain of the last two weeks was—to her—unthinkable. If she was swatting away at anything that day, it was at the Satan in me.

That afternoon was hot. I sat upstairs in my bedroom, where I'd been banished, the morning air upstairs gradually weakening in midsummer's heat. I lay down for a while. I sat on the chair at the head of the stairs and felt the sweat around the back of my neck. And then I stood on the stairs, ready to go down, thinking that I needed to tell her that those three bags of straw weren't what she thought they were.

But I didn't. What I'd already done convinced me that I was guilty, even if this time I wasn't. I knew I deserved at least some of her anger. So I sat upstairs in the dank heat and hoped she'd find out some way that this time she was wrong.

An hour later she came up with a glass of lemonade. She was crying. That was the third time in two weeks I'd seen and heard my mother cry. She'd phoned another mother and found out that we didn't steal the straw. She'd hit me without cause, banished me to my room without reason, without listening to my story. I'd been guilty in her eyes, and she knew that she'd been wrong.

She handed me a fifty-cent piece. Some time before, I'd told her that I wanted to buy a scrapbook from the variety store, so she placed that heavy coin in the palm of my hand and told me to go out and buy it. She wasn't trying to buy back my love. I knew, even then, that that fifty cents was her penance, and I accepted it that way.

The tears came this third time from yet another source. This time they were born from guilt and shame and the need for forgiveness.

Parents of fussy three-year-olds spend no small amount of time reassuring themselves that some-day their kids will be old enough not to need them twenty-four hours a day. Parents of thirteen-year-olds like to remember the finally quiet nights when their kids slept innocently in five-year cribs. To parents, a child's constant dependence can some-times be an insufferable burden; but independence can be crippling. Just recently a mother of nine told me that saying goodbye to her oldest was just like giving birth all over again.

I'm not sure how much taller I grew in those two weeks when my mother cried three times, but I knew that I grew in the inevitable direction all children must—toward independence and away from my parents. Before that time they had never considered their son capable of stealing, of breaking the fifth commandment spoken so clearly every Sunday morning of his life. To know for a fact that he was something else meant a painful separation, meant seeing me as someone whose behavior could not be guarded and controlled as it had been when as a toddler I stood outside in a diaper and sucked on clothespins while Mom hung out the wash. I was becoming someone more than simply my parents' little boy. I was opening the calendar myself to the years of discretion.

And I knew it. The first time my mother had cried, sadness and disappointment prompted her tears. The second time, it was anger and pain. But the third time, the time I remember best of the three, her tears flowed from her mistake, her culpability, her error, her sin. And I knew it. With that fifty cents, she was asking me to think of her as someone more than simply my mother, some-one born in Eve's own sin, prone to weakness, not unlike the self I saw in the image of a kid become a thief.

In those two weeks, both of us changed. In her eyes, I'd become someone more than simply her child and in my eyes she'd become someone more than simply my mother.

That third bout of tears was the greatest of the three, because, in admitting weakness, she was illustrating her strength. She was strong enough to be humble, to admit to her humanity's loose ends, and, in so doing, she gave me a model of the divinity inherent in human forgiveness. She showed me the possibilities of her humanity and thus defined what it meant to be a wretched creature of sin who is, oddly enough, endowed with the image of God.

That day I saw my mother as a struggling human being. To a struggling kid, I could see no better vision.

So today I thank her for those tears.

"My Mother's Tears," by James C. Schaap, *The Banner*, Sept. 15, 1986, pp. 12–13

Getting Rid of God-Talk

Third, when we explain the Christian message, we should learn to do so in plain language—hopefully in fresh and creative ways. Few things turn off people faster or alienate them more easily than God-talk. Without realizing it we use words or cliches that have a correct understanding only among Christians. At an evangelistic dorm talk a non-Christian student asked me, "What does it mean to be a Christian?"

A Christian student who really desired the other student to understand replied, "It means you have to be washed in the blood of the Lamb." The first student paled and looked confused. The Christian continued, "That way you will be sanctified and redeemed."

Another student seeking to help his Christian brother said, "And the fellowship is so neat. Praise the Lord! You really get into the Word and get such a blessing." By the end of the conversation one would have thought these Christians came from another planet.

To the world, evangelical cliches are often either red flags or else the meaning is imprecise. Of course we must not dispense with biblical words and concepts. Instead we need to develop fresh and relevant ways to express what they mean. Frequently I will describe what a word means, then say, "That's what the Bible means when it talks about sin." If we do it in that sequence we can arouse curiosity and diffuse defenses.

For example, I was walking out of an English class one day after the professor had discussed the question, "Is the human dilemma tragic?" A fellow student and I began talking about what he had said.

"You know, the Bible says the human situation is tragic. . . ."

"Oh, I know," she interrupted. "You Christians say we are all sinners."

"But Joan," I responded, "do you know why? The Bible says it's because something very, very precious has been broken. If we weren't so significant, if we didn't have so much meaning, then it wouldn't be so sad. It's only when something precious has been broken that we can say, 'How tragic!' That brokenness is what the Bible calls sin. That's why God hates it so much. It caused something extremely precious to become dehumanized."

Here are other common Christian terms we should learn to express in fresh ways: *grace, salvation, justification, sanctification, regeneration, redemption, born again.* And the following phrases also need our creative touch: *having a personal relationship with Jesus, asking Jesus to come into your heart, feeling Jesus in your heart, getting a blessing, getting into the Word.* Your Christian group may well have other obscure phrases meaningful to only the initiated. Learn to translate them.

Out of the Saltshaker by Rebecca M. Pippert, pp. 130–132

Paul's Conversion

Take the conversion of St. Paul. So far from its being exceptional, I believe it is meant by St. Luke to be normative for all Christians everywhere. That is why he gives us three accounts of it. Not, of course, that the shattering heavenly vision, the blindness, the prostration on the ground and the voice like thunder are to be expected again. They are the mere external trappings of Paul's conversion. But the principles lie deeper. This encounter with Christ touched Paul at every level of his being. *His mind* was informed and illuminated: Jesus was not, as he had thought, accursed, but was the Lord. *His conscience* was reached: he faced up to the fact that he had been kicking against the pricks. *His emotions* were stirred as he saw the implications of his rebellion against Christ. But this was a mere incidental on the way to his will, Christ's real goal. *His will* was bent in trusting surrender to Jesus who had called him, and who was from henceforth to be Lord of his life. And in consequence *his life* was transformed: in direction, immediately, and in achievement as time went on. His supreme aim henceforth was to live for his Redeemer: "I was not disobedient to the heavenly vision, but declared first to those at Damascus then at Jerusalem . . . that they should repent and turn to God" (Acts 26:19–20).

This conversion of St. Paul is rightly called in 1 Timothy 1:16 a pattern for subsequent believers. Despite the enormous variety of temperaments, backgrounds and capacities of the men reached by the gospel in the early Church, an illuminated mind, a quickened conscience, a humbled grateful heart, a yielded will and a changed life were the common factors in the conversion of them all.

Evangelism in the Early Church by Michael Green, p. 161

SEVEN

LEADING TO DECISION

If we follow some of the basic suggestions in this book—building friendships, learning to listen, and talking about our personal relationship with Christ—it's likely that at some time one or more of our non-Christian friends will ask some basic questions. "O.K. I like what I see in your life. I like what you're saying. Now how do I become a Christian? How do I become right with God?" And it's vitally important that we know how to answer.

Some Christians are especially gifted for evangelism. Research by C. Peter Wagner suggests that 10 percent of the members in a typical congregation are able to present the gospel to unbelievers in a clear and meaningful way that calls for response. But while not all of us have the spiritual gift of evangelism, we all *are* called to be witnesses. And we all will occasionally find the opportunity to lead someone to Christ. When someone calls out for help, we must be prepared to respond and to invite that person to join God's family.

In his book *Evangelism as a Lifestyle* Jim Petersen remarks that he has been on enough guilt trips over evangelism to travel around the world twice. Some of that guilt that Jim and many of us feel may be unnecessary, because not all of us have the spiritual gift of evangelism. But even those of us who do *not* have that special gift are without excuse if God gives us the opportunity to be the instrument of new life and we refuse to use that moment to bring about the rebirth of a friend.

The focus in this book is on living beautifully and witnessing to God's goodness in a natural way. We build friendships without fail—conversion or not—until death or circumstances beyond our control pull us apart. But friendships should never make us impotent when the Holy Spirit is making a new creation before our eyes.

The Voyage of the Dawn Treader

Eustace was an obnoxious little boy whose selfish and thoughtless behavior so hardened him that he eventually turned into a dragon. In the following excerpt from The Voyage of the Dawn Treader, *Eustace tells his friend Edmund how he changed back from a dragon into a boy.*

Read C.S. Lewis's classic description of the conversion of Eustace the dragon. Then discuss or jot down some of your ideas about the author's insights into what happens when spiritual conversion takes place.

[Edmund and Eustace] went to the rocks and sat down, looking out across the bay while the sky got paler and paler and the stars disappeared except for one very bright one low down and near the horizon. . . .

"I want to tell you how I stopped being [a dragon," Eustace began.]

"Fire ahead," said Edmund.

"Well, last night I was more miserable than ever . . . . I was lying awake and wondering what on earth would become of me. And then—but, mind you, it may have been all a dream. I don't know."

"Go on," said Edmund, with considerable patience.

"Well, anyway, I looked up and saw the very last thing I expected: a huge lion coming slowly towards me. And one queer thing—there was no moon last night, but there was moonlight where the lion was. So it came nearer and nearer. I was terribly afraid of it. You may think that, being a dragon, I could have knocked any lion out easily enough. But it wasn't that kind of fear. I wasn't afraid of it eating me, I was just afraid of it—if you can understand. Well, it came closer up to me and looked straight into my eyes. And I shut my eyes tight. But that wasn't any good because it told me to follow it."

"You mean it spoke?"

"I don't know. Now that you mention it, I don't think it did. But it told me all the same. And I knew I'd have to do what it told me, so I got up and followed it. And it led me a long way into the mountains. And there was always this moonlight over and around the lion wherever we went. So at last we came to the top of a mountain I'd never seen before and on the top of this mountain there was a garden—trees and fruit and everything. In the middle of it there was a well.

"I knew it was a well because you could see the water bubbling up from the bottom of it: but it was a lot bigger than most wells—like a very big, round bath with marble steps going down into it. The water was as clear as anything, and I thought if I could get in there and bathe, it would ease the pain in my leg. But the lion told me I must undress first. Mind you, I don't know if he said any words out loud or not.

"I was just going to say that I couldn't undress because I hadn't any clothes on when I suddenly thought that dragons are snaky sort of things and snakes can cast their skins. Oh, of course, thought I, that's what the lion means. So I started scratching myself and my scales began coming off all over the place. And then I scratched a little deeper and, instead of just scales coming off here and there, my whole skin started peeling off beautifully, like it does after an illness, or as if I was a banana. In a minute or two I just stepped out of it. I could see it lying there beside me, looking rather nasty. It was a most lovely feeling. So I started to go down into the well for my bath.

"But just as I was going to put my foot into the water I looked down and saw that it was all hard and rough and wrinkled and scaly just as it had been before. Oh, that's all right, said I, it only means I had another smaller suit on underneath the first one, and I'll have to get out of it too. So I scratched and tore again and this under skin peeled off beautifully and out I stepped and left it lying beside the other one and went down to the well for my bath.

"Well, exactly the same thing happened again. And I thought to myself, oh dear, how ever many skins have I got to take off? For I was longing to bathe my leg. So I scratched away for the third time and got off a third skin, just like the two others, and stepped out of it. But as soon as I looked at myself in the water, I knew it had been no good.

"Then the lion said—but I don't know if it spoke—you will have to let me undress you. I was afraid of his claws, I can tell you, but I was pretty nearly desperate now. So I just lay flat down on my back to let him do it.

"The very first tear he made was so deep that I thought it had gone right into my heart. And when he began pulling the skin off, it hurt worse than anything I've ever felt. The only thing that made me able to bear it was just the pleasure of feeling the stuff peel off. You know—if you've ever picked the scab off a sore place. It hurts like billy—oh but it is such fun to see it coming away."

"I know exactly what you mean," said Edmund.

"Well, he peeled the beastly stuff right off—just as I thought I'd done it myself the other three times, only they hadn't hurt—and there it was lying on the grass: only ever so much thicker, and darker, and more knobbly looking than the others had been. And there was I as smooth and soft as a peeled switch and smaller than I had been. Then he caught hold of me—I didn't like that much for I was very tender underneath now that I'd no skin on—and threw me into the water. It smarted like anything but only for a moment. After that it became perfectly delicious and as soon as I started swimming and splashing I found that all the pain had gone from my arm. And then I saw why. I'd turned into a boy again. You'd think me simply phoney if I told you how I felt about my own arms. I know they've no muscle and are pretty mouldy compared with Caspian's, but I was so glad to see them.

"After a bit the lion took me out and dressed me—"

"Dressed you. With his paws?"

"Well, I don't exactly remember that bit. But he did somehow or other: in new clothes—the same I've got on now, as a matter of fact. And then suddenly I was back here. Which is what makes me think it must have been a dream."

"No. It wasn't a dream," said Edmund.

"Why not?"

"Well, there are the clothes, for one thing. And you have been—well, un-dragoned, for another."

"What do you think it was, then?" asked Eustace.

"I think you've seen Aslan," said Edmund.

The Voyage of the Dawn Treader by C.S. Lewis, pp. 87–91

Bible Study: Matthew 13:3–8

Can you identify a friend who at this time appears to be "good soil"? If so, can you think of a way to extend a gospel invitation to that person in the near future? Why or why not?

A farmer went out to sow his seed. As he was scattering the seed, some fell along the path, and the birds came and ate it up. Some fell on rocky places, where it did not have much soil. It sprang up quickly, because the soil was shallow. But when the sun came up, the plants were scorched, and they withered because they had no root. Other seed fell among the thorns, which grew up and choked the plants. Still other seed fell on good soil, where it produced a crop—a hundred, sixty or thirty times what was sown.
Matthew 13:3–8

Transitional Questions

At some point in one of our discussions with a friend, he may be ready to make a faith commitment but may not be sure what to say or how to go about it. As witnesses we must try to be sensitive to such a transition and learn to ask the right questions—questions that will lead our friend to Christ.

A pastor illustrates one way of handling a transition. He explains that he was counseling two reforming alcoholics and discussed religious matters with them often. One evening he tried to explain his faith again, but the women had so many doubts and questions about the things he told them that he had pretty much given up hope of any real progress as the discussion came to a close. Then, after an awkward silence one of the women said, "Well, I don't know where we go from here." Something in her manner stirred the pastor to pursue her comment. He asked, "Are you saying you would like to commit yourself to faith in Christ but don't know how to get started?" Both women responded positively, and the pastor was then able to suggest that they pray with him and that they commit themselves to begin a relationship with Jesus (adapted from the leader's guide to *Basic Training for Disciples: Training for Witness* by Carl Schroder).

Joseph Aldrich recommends another approach that we might use when our friends seem close to decision, something he calls the "pilgrimage question": "Bill, at what point are you in your spiritual pilgrimage?" The question allows Bill to talk about a process without actually saying yes or no to whether he is a Christian. Ambiguous enough to allow several levels of biblical sophistication, this question may help the witness gauge whether this is an appropriate time for a call to decision.

Try to recall examples of transition times— times when people were knocking on the door but were not completely able or free to ask you to lead them through the decision process.

Qualifying Question

After going through the gospel outline and before asking directly whether your friend wants to receive eternal life through Jesus Christ, you have to make sure you've communicated effectively. James Kennedy says this is the time to ask a qualifying question: "Does this make sense to you?"

Asking this qualifying question helps you avoid the possibility of a premature commitment and lets you know whether your friend understands the gospel offer. If it becomes evident that he or she does not understand, repeat again the main points and then again ask the qualifying question. Always ask "Does this make sense to you?" Don't ask "What doesn't make sense?"

If, after review, your friend indicates that some matters are still fuzzy, don't ask for a commitment; instead, invite your friend to do some additional study with you. Make an appointment for the first session.

However, if your friend responds, "Yes, I understand the gospel" and you are encouraged by the tone of the response, then ask for a commitment: "Is there any reason why you wouldn't want to receive Jesus Christ right now?"

It's often not easy to determine exactly when a person is ready to make a commitment to Christ, but the qualifying question may help. Think about other signals that might help you know if your friend is ready to make a commitment.

Thought Questions

1. Research indicates that people are often attracted to the gospel for selfish reasons. They may be trapped in terrible problems at home or at work and are envious of the serenity they see in their Christian friends. Obviously we shouldn't exploit such selfish reasons when presenting the gospel. But shouldn't we try to work though a person's problems before seeking a commitment from him or her? Do you agree with Jim Petersen's conclusion:

We need to accept the non-Christian as he is, go for the cure, and then *help him pick his way through the things that are destroying him. Whenever we get this sequence turned around, we become reformers rather than offerers of true healing.*

Evangelism as a Lifestyle by Jim Petersen, p. 93

2. People God places in our path often do not deeply feel a need for forgiveness. Frequently they suppress any awareness of being alienated from God. The parable of the prodigal son indicates that until the son tried all the options and found them wanting, he did not return home. Can we conclude that sinners generally will not come home until they have "bottomed out," as did the prodigal?

The Shocking Alternative

In Mere Christianity *C.S. Lewis makes his well-known argument for the uniqueness of Jesus. Read the selection over and then talk about these questions:*

▶1. How does Lewis's description of Christ make you feel? What impact might this line of thought have on a non-Christian friend?

▶2. How might you introduce this piece to a non-Christian friend?

▶3. What follow-up questions might you ask?

Among the Jews there suddenly turns up a man who goes about talking as if He was God. He claims to forgive sins. He says He has always existed. He says He is coming to judge the world at the end of time. Now let us get this clear. Among Pantheists, like the Indians, anyone might say that he was a part of God, or one with God: there would be nothing very odd about it. But this man, since He was a Jew, could not mean that kind of God. God, in their language, meant the Being outside the world who had made it and was infinitely different from anything else. And when you have grasped that, you will see that what this man said was, quite simply, the most shocking thing that has ever been uttered by human lips.

One part of the claim tends to slip past us unnoticed because we have heard it so often that we no longer see what it amounts to. I mean the claim to forgive sins: any sins. Now unless the speaker is God, this is really so preposterous as to be comic. We can all understand how a man forgives offenses against himself. You tread on my toe and I forgive you, you steal my money and I forgive you. But what should we make of a man, himself unrobbed and untrodden on, who announced that he forgave you for treading on other men's toes and stealing other men's money? Asinine fatuity is the kindest description we should give of his conduct. Yet this is what Jesus did. He told people that their sins were forgiven, and never waited to consult all the other people whom their sins had undoubtedly injured. He unhesitatingly behaved as if He was the party chiefly concerned, the person chiefly offended in all offenses. This makes sense only if He really was the God whose laws are broken and whose love is wounded in every sin. In the mouth of any speaker who is not God, these words would imply what I can only regard as a silliness and conceit unrivalled by any other character in history.

Yet (and this is the strange, significant thing) even His enemies when they read the Gospels, do not usually get the impression of silliness and conceit. Still less do unprejudiced readers. Christ says that He is "humble and meek" and we believe Him; not noticing that, if He were merely a man, humility and meekness are the very last characteristics we could attribute to some of His sayings.

I am trying here to prevent anyone saying the really foolish thing that people often say about Him: "I'm ready to accept Jesus as a great moral teacher, but I don't accept His claim to be God." That is one thing we must not say. A man who was merely a man and said the sort of things Jesus said would not be a great moral teacher. He would either be a lunatic—on a level with the man who says he is a poached egg—or else he would be the Devil of Hell. You must make your choice. Either this man was, and is, the Son of God: or else a madman or something worse. You can shut Him up for a fool, you can spit at Him and kill Him as a demon; or you can fall at His feet and call Him Lord and God. But let us not come with any patronizing nonsense about His being a great human teacher. He has not left that open to us. He did not intend to.

Mere Christianity by C.S. Lewis, pp. 54–56

Two Gospel Presentations

Some of you already may have memorized and used a specific evangelism method, such as the Four Spiritual Laws, Coral Ridge, Bridge to New Life, and so on. Others have had no experience with such a systematic approach to evangelism.

Well-equipped witnesses *should* be able to use effectively at least two evangelism methods. This book teaches the Roman Road method, which involves an open Bible, and the Bridge to New Life method, which uses simple diagrams to explain the gospel.

The Roman Road

With this method of presenting the gospel, witnesses use a series of verses from the book of Romans. Either write the locations of the verses in the front of your Bible or simply underline them in Romans. Memorizing the location of the passages will allow you to use the method with any Bible (not just your personal copy).

As you read through the verses with a friend, you can stop and talk about each one, leading that person through the progression from human sin to God's provision to our response.

This week take time to study the context of the passages from Romans so you'll be able to explain them better.

Our Sin

Romans 3:23 For all have sinned and fall short of the glory of God.

Sin's Penalty

Romans 6:23 For the wages of sin is death, but the gift of God is eternal life in Christ Jesus our Lord.

God's Provision

Romans 5:8 But God demonstrates his own love for us in this: While we were still sinners, Christ died for us.

Romans 5:1 Therefore, since we have been justified through faith, we have peace with God through our Lord Jesus Christ.

Our Response

Romans 10:9 If you confess with your mouth, "Jesus is Lord," and believe in your heart that God raised him from the dead, you will be saved.

Our New Life

Romans 12:1–2 Therefore, I urge you, brothers, in view of God's mercy, to offer your bodies as living sacrifices, holy and pleasing to God—this is your spiritual act of worship. Do not conform any longer to the pattern of this world, but be transformed by the renewing of your mind. Then you will be able to test and approve what God's will is—his good, pleasing, and perfect will.

The Bridge to New Life

The "Bridge" method of presenting the good news of salvation is one of the easiest to remember and explain. Once you've memorized the basic steps of the approach (outlined below), you can use it almost anywhere with only a pen and a piece of paper (restaurant napkins work fine!).

Your presentation with the bridge need not be complex and need not contain all the elements we have described on these pages. The important thing is that the person you are witnessing to understands the reality of the separation between God and his people and the centrality of Christ's atonement. As you talk together, you can present a clear picture of the gospel through continued reference on the right side to God's love and provision and on the left side to human need. The steps follow:

1. Today people are troubled by the world in which they live. But there is good news from God. You can know God's love and discover purpose for your life (John 3:16; 10:10).

2. People's own choices have resulted in separation from God. Thus they cannot know God's love and purpose for their lives. A great gap separates people from God.

Only God (holy) can give us real purpose and meaning in life. People (sinful) try to live without God or reach him through good deeds, the occult, drugs, philosophy, and the like. Their best efforts fall short of God's perfect standards (Isa. 64:6; Rom. 3:23; 6:23).

3. Jesus Christ is the only bridge between humanity and God.

Christ lived a perfect life and then died on a cross, taking the punishment for all of our sins on himself. He did this because he loves us and wants to close the gap between us and God (John 14:6; 1 Pet. 3:16; 1 Tim. 2:5).

4. You can cross the bridge by personally receiving Jesus Christ as Savior and Lord. Only then will you experience God's love and purpose in your life.

You can put Christ in control by repenting (1 John 1:9) and by having faith in God's promises (John 1:12; Eph. 2:8).

Suggested prayer:

Dear Jesus, I confess my sins. Please forgive them. I ask that you be my Savior. I also ask that you become the Lord of my life. On the basis of your promises in the Bible, I thank you for this new life. Amen.

REFLECTIONS

The 25th Man

One man I know accepted Christ, and his life changed radically overnight. For several years he was a glowing witness for Christ. Suddenly, the bottom dropped out. He returned to his former life. His family and friends were deeply disappointed, and their non-Christian acquaintances ridiculed his professional conversion. But after seven years, I saw that man come back into the fellowship of the Lord again and begin to recapture the vitality of commitment.

Another friend of mine, a young pastor, was used to lead a hardened criminal to Christ in a county jail. This man told him, "Now preacher, don't get the big head because I have accepted Christ. You are just the twenty-fifth man."

"What do you mean, I'm the twenty-fifth man?" my friend asked.

"Well," he said, "I can think of at least twenty-four others who have witnessed to me about Christ. And it was the effect of all this together that finally led me to Christ. You just happened to be the twenty-fifth."

Sometimes God works quickly, immediately. Sometimes slowly, patiently. Sometimes we may be the first person, sometimes the fifth, sometimes the twenty-fifth in the process. Not everyone with whom we share Christ will respond. Not all of those who respond will do so sincerely. Not all of those whom we think are sincere will last. Some will go up and down. But as we have patient faith in the power of the gospel, as we continue patiently to share, we will see enough lives transformed to see that the gospel really does have power.

Good News Is for Sharing by Leighton Ford, p. 49

How to Be Convincing

People often ask, "If Christianity is true, why do the majority of intelligent people not believe it?" The answer is precisely the same as the reason the majority of unintelligent people don't believe it. They don't want to because they're unwilling to accept the moral demands it would make on their lives. We can take a horse to water but we can't make him drink. A person must be willing to believe before he ever will believe. There isn't a thing you or I can do with a man who, despite all evidence to the contrary, insists that black is white.

We ourselves must be convinced about the truth we proclaim. Otherwise we won't be at all convincing to other people. We must be able to say confidently with Peter, ". . . . we did not follow cleverly devised myths when we made known to you the power and coming of our Lord Jesus Christ" (2 Pet. 1:16). Then our witness will ring with authority, conviction, and the power of the Holy Spirit.

How to Give Away Your Faith by Paul Little, p. 81

The Bomb

Then came the bomb. She suddenly looked straight at me and said, "I feel like God is over there," as she gestured with her hand, "and I am over here. I've really wanted to know God all of my life. But how do I bridge the gap? What would I do if I wanted to become a Christian?"

I stared at her in disbelief. No one had ever asked me that question. I not only felt inept, but terrified that at this crucial moment God wouldn't come through. I had wondered what I would do if this ever happened. But the same scenario had always plagued me. The person would ask me to become a Christian. I would say, "Fine. Let's just pray together and ask God to come into your life." We would pray and then she would say, "Ah, Becky, I hate to say this. But . . . . um . . . . I don't feel any different. I mean I feel just exactly the way I did before we prayed." I would secretly think, Oh, *how* embarrassing! But I would say, "Well, listen. Why don't we just try it again." We would pray again, but then she would tell me she still felt the same. Then I would say, "Well, look, it's Saturday. Maybe weekends are a busy time. Let's try it again next week." And I would escape as fast as I could. Just the thought of facing such an episode made me quake. And here was Mary, asking me to help her, immediately, directly, and *now*.

"Well, what should I do?" Mary asked me.

"Ahhhh, well, I guess you could, um, pray," I answered weakly.

"I don't know how. What should I say?" she persisted.

"Well, ah, you could tell God what you told me," I stammered.

"Okay. *When* should I tell him?" she asked.

For the first time I brightened.

"You can tell him the *minute* you get home," I replied, leaping from my chair and ushering her quickly out of the room. "As soon as you get home just tell him everything," I said as I pushed her through the front door. "And read the last chapter of Stott's book on how to become a Christian," I shouted as she walked down the steps looking a bit bewildered.

I felt miserable. God wasn't asking John Stott to lead Mary to faith. He was asking me. And I felt I had failed. I had been ashamed and embarrassed. I felt inadequate and unqualified to help Mary. But most of all, I lacked the faith and the guts to believe God actually would come through and that he could use me. So I tried to forget the entire incident. After all, maybe Mary had just had a bad day. She was probably feeling emotional and would have been terribly embarrassed later if I had done anything anyway.

The next day Ruth returned from a trip. As I recounted my experience with Mary to her, she became more and more excited. Before I could even finish she interrupted, her eyes shining, and she said, "Oh, Becky, then you led her to Christ, right?"

And I answered, a bit subdued, "No, actually, I led her out the door."

It was the only time I ever saw Ruth unable to cover her disappointment. "Becky! Why not? You've led other friends to Christ, haven't you?"

"Ah, well, let's see now. It's kind of hard to remember. I guess, ah, *actually*—ah . . . . no."

Mary returned to my apartment a few days later. I was amazed to hear her account of what happened after she left me and amused by how she described it. She told Ruth in a somewhat exasperated tone, "Well, I asked Becky what to do and she told me to go home. But at least she said to read the last chapter of that book. Now listen, I really do believe this stuff and I prayed that prayer at the end of the book. Does that mean I'm 'in'?"

Ruth assured her that she was indeed a child of God. But I remained somewhat skeptical and waited to see the results. The results, by the way, were that Mary grew steadily and is a Christian to this day. I need also to say that since that experience nearly ten years ago, I have rarely seen someone convert to Christ as quickly as she did. God had been working on her a long time before I ever met her. But seemingly quick conversions are the exception, in my experience, not the norm.

Out of the Saltshaker by Rebecca M. Pippert, pp. 21–23

Never Easier Than Now

There is always an urgency when helping individuals to find Christ. They are to seek the Lord while he may be found and to call upon him while he is near. In my experience there are certain times—probably not very many—when God is especially to be found and when Christ is very near. Each opportunity is therefore a critical time, and needs prayerful and sensitive handling. Time over again I have seen people brought to the very brink of decision, and then, for one reason or another, they have pulled away a little. All too often a hardening process begins to set in, and they never seem to get so close to the Lord again. Therefore gently and prayerfully we need to persuade an individual to make this personal commitment to Christ. Often I say, "You will never find it easier than you will now"—which I am convinced is true. At the same time undue pressure could be disastrous, leading perhaps to a spiritual abortion. Once a person understands what to do, I usually ask some such question as, "Would you like me to lead you in a personal prayer, which you can make your own, to help you to ask Christ into your life; or would you prefer to read something, and then take the step on your own when you feel you are ready?" The alternative is a helpful way of not forcing a person into a corner. If he wishes to read and pray on his own, I will encourage him to let me know as soon as he has done this, partly as a seal to his own personal commitment and partly because he will need much guidance and encouragement after that initial step. If he prefers to pray with me then and there, I will sometimes explain first what I am about to pray, and then, if he is happy with that, lead him in a personal prayer which he can make his own, silently or aloud, phrase for phrase, after me.

I Believe in Evangelism by David Watson, p. 112

REFLECTIONS

The Gift of God

Saving faith is not a gift of the evangelist to his unsaved hearer: "it is the gift of God" (Eph. 2:8). No evangelist ever imparted faith in Christ to a single soul; it is wrought in human hearts by the Holy Spirit, for "no man can say that Jesus is the Lord, but by the Holy Ghost" (1 Cor. 12:3). No sinner was ever converted by an evangelist; the author of conversion is God. Scripture accounts for Lydia's conversion, not by saying that she lifted the latch of her heart from within, nor yet by relating that the great apostle by his convincing reasoning and eloquent appeal softened her heart, but by insisting that the Lord opened her heart so that she attended to the things which were spoken of Paul (Acts 16:14).

It was in the full realization of the evangelist's complete dependence on God for the effectiveness of his labors that the church's most celebrated missionary wrote: "Who then is Paul, and who is Apollos, but ministers by whom ye believed, even as the Lord gave to every man? I have planted, Apollos watered; but God gave the increase. So then neither is he that planteth any thing, neither he that watereth; but God that giveth the increase" (1 Cor. 3:5–7).

It is the profound teaching of Holy Scripture that the ultimate explanation for a given person's coming to faith lies in God's sovereign election of him from the foundation of the world unto salvation. In the saying of Jesus, "Many are called, but few are chosen" (Matt. 22:14), it is plainly implicit that of the many who are called by the gospel the few who believe do so because they are divinely chosen to that end from eternity. And Luke said in so many words that in response to the preaching of Paul and Barnabas to the Gentiles at Antioch in Pisidia "as many as were ordained to eternal life believed" (Acts 13:48). God did the ordaining. God also made good his ordaining by the imparting of saving faith.

God-Centered Evangelism by R.B. Kuiper, pp. 189–190

The Christian's primary calling is to witness, to be a light, to play the music. His strategy is low pressure, long range. He is a seed planter who knows when to plant the seeds! He thoroughly trusts God to bring a harvest. This does not mean he is lazy. It simply means he knows you have to plant seed, cultivate it, water it, and wait for the harvest.

Life-Style Evangelism by Joseph C. Aldrich, pp. 84–85

EIGHT

FACING OUR FEARS

Almost all Christians have their own list of reasons for not witnessing. "People won't be interested anyway." "Witnessing demands more knowledge than I have." "It'll threaten our friendship." "I'm not good enough at quoting Scripture."

All these excuses are cover-ups for the one barrier that stands at the very top: "I'm afraid. I don't have the courage."

To some extent all of us are anxious about the unknown. "Will I make a fool of myself?" "How will I cope if my friends are offended?" "What will others think of me?" Witnessing in natural settings alleviates much of our anxiety; the more friendly our relationships, the less pressure we ought to feel. But even in normal circumstances, most of us cannot escape being somewhat anxious.

Fear is mutual, of course. Non-Christians carry around stereotypes about Bible-bashing believers. And sometimes they're right. We make the mistake of acting holier-than-thou when we should be "the aroma of Christ among those who are being saved and those who are perishing. To the one we [should be] the smell of death; to the other, the fragrance of life" (2 Cor. 2:15–16).

Somehow we seldom live up to this biblical image. We're concerned that non-Christians seem to ignore the sin that is destroying them. Yet we instinctively hold back. Our anxiety over witness never entirely disappears.

Even the early apostles had that problem. The intrepid Paul came to the Corinthians "with much trembling" (1 Cor. 2:3). The brash Peter was scared on occasion. Ananias refused at first to see Paul even when the Holy Spirit directly ordered him to do so (Acts 9:10–19). Practice and experience will alleviate some of our fears, but none of us need presume that we are fearless. Why think ourselves superior to such great agents of God's work as Paul, Peter, and Ananias?

101

Anxiety Scale

Score yourself on the anxiety chart, indicating how you react to each of the ten situations. (*Note:* No one ever scores 0 on this test. That should tell you something about anxiety!)

When you are finished, add up your score from the ten graphs and evaluate your own weaknesses and fears as you consider the questions below:

▶1. Does anything in your responses suggest that meeting people is difficult for you? If so, how might you improve in that area?

▶2. Do you have any general suggestions about what we can do to alleviate our fear of witnessing?

There is a careless streak in love . . . . It is risky to put oneself out for another, to go out of one's way to help another person—when one is not sure of how to do it well. One may be misunderstood, deceived, hurt. We could flub our overtures of love and end up looking ridiculous. Moved by love, however, we overpower our fear and take the risk.
Love Within Limits by Lewis Smedes, p. 105

NO FEAR "No sweat."		NORMAL "OK, but not total joy."		SCARED TO DEATH "No way."

1. swimming in a lake

0	1	2	3	4

2. visiting a sick person in the hospital

0	1	2	3	4

3. telling friends what I received for Christmas

0	1	2	3	4

4. handing out tracts on a street corner

0	1	2	3	4

5. going up to a new person at church and introducing myself

0	1	2	3	4

6. visiting the dentist

0	1	2	3	4

7. speaking out at the PTA meeting

0	1	2	3	4

8. telling a friend why I am a Christian

0	1	2	3	4

9. closing in prayer without warning at a public meeting

0	1	2	3	4

10. walking around your own home at night with lights out

0	1	2	3	4

Adapted from *Growing as a Caring Community* by William C. Cline, pp. 9–10

Bible Study: 2 Corinthians 4:7

During Paul's day it was common to conceal treasures in clay jars that had little or no value. Such jars—perhaps comparable to today's peanut butter or jelly jars—did not attract attention to themselves. As other translations say, they were "pots of earthenware," "common jars," and "perishable containers." The treasure described in verse 6 ("knowledge of the glory of God") is held in just such earthen vessels.

According to an old story, when Jesus returned to heaven, he was asked how he could guarantee that his work on earth would continue. "I have entrusted it to ordinary people," Jesus replied. "There's no other provision. I'm counting on them." We are the clay jars—the ordinary, frail, and unworthy people who hold the treasures of God. How good it is to know that the power of the gospel comes from God, not from us (v. 7)! Knowing this can make us less preoccupied with ourselves and less fearful of failure.

Apply Paul's teaching about "treasure in clay pots" to various biblical examples: Jacob (Gen. 27:18–29), Amos (Amos 1:1; 7:14–15), Matthew (Matt. 9:9–13), Nathanael (John 1:45–49), Ananias (Acts 9:10–19), and Lydia (Acts 16:13–15). For each of these ordinary people God used to do his work, discuss the following questions:

▶1. In what ways was this biblical person ordinary?

▶2. How did God use this person?

But we have this treasure in jars of clay to show that this all-surpassing power is from God and not from us.

2 Corinthians 4:7

104

Thought Questions

▶1. John Madden, tough man of the National Football League before his retirement, is afraid of airplanes. During a busy football season Madden's role as a sports announcer demands a lot of travel. So Madden spends nearly all of his spare time on trains, criss-crossing the United States.

A friend of mine is terrified of snakes. He's been afraid for the past fifty years and undoubtedly will stay that way.

Although we work to overcome most of our fears, John Madden and my friend illustrate that we feel no pressing need to overcome *some* typical fears. For example, when we fear airplanes or dentists or snakes or spiders or heights, we may take some good-natured ribbing, but we expect others to overlook our phobias.

May we allow witnessing to fall into this category of overlookable phobias? Or is fear no excuse when it comes to telling others about Christ? Explain.

▶2. Sometimes we fear witnessing because we are intensely aware of our own shortcomings. We worry that others will see us as we really are and reject our testimony as empty words. This story from *Of Cabbages and Kings* by Jacob D. Eppinga may help put this fear in perspective:

My father was a builder. He was handy with tools. And so, with plenty of tools and wood available, I would sometimes construct boats or birdhouses. But my hands didn't match. I was totally without talent in this regard, whereas my father seemed born with tools in his hands. Nevertheless, I well remember how he would look at my latest monstrosity, full of bent nails, and commend my production. It made me feel good . . . . warm and secure inside.

It makes me think of our Lord. It is too bad that we readily see him as a critical judge rather than as a loving father. We come to him with our poor bumbling efforts, full of bent nails. Our very best productions must look pathetic in his sight . . . . Instead he says to his children whom he loves, "Well done, thou good and faithful servant." Imagine. A compliment from God himself!

In *Evangelism as a Lifestyle* Jim Petersen says much the same thing: "It is my observation that any Christian who is sincerely seeking to walk with God in spite of all his flaws, reflects something of Christ."

Should we fear witnessing because of our shortcomings? What do Eppinga and Petersen have to say about this (see also 2 Cor. 12:9)? Remember that a common complaint among non-Christians is that Christians talk a good game but really aren't much different from non-Christians.

▶3. Perhaps we are afraid to witness because we worry that we will be "won over" to the side of unbelief by the very persons we are trying to win over to Christianity. We feel uncomfortable and threatened around non-Christians. What guarantee, if any, do we have that we will be lifted up by the power of Christ rather than brought down by the power of Satan (see 1 John 4:4)?

▶4. Fear of the unknown is often the root cause of our anxiety about witnessing. Why, then, are we sometimes afraid to witness to our relatives? Shouldn't we be close enough to them that we need not worry about unpredictable responses? Why do we so often ignore the uncommitted in our families?

▶5. Perhaps we worry about lacking the spiritual strength to perform well in a crisis witness situation. In physical emergencies we may experience a rush of adrenalin that enables us to perform outstanding feats. For example, I recently read about a one-hundred-twenty-pound woman who pushed up an overturned car so her parents could escape. But does the same thing happen in spiritual emergencies? May we expect unusual spiritual strength when caught in a difficult witnessing situation? Comment.

His Master's Voice

This is an account of how Hans Uittenbosch, a harbor chaplain in Montreal, courageously confronted a captain whose ship was full of sick and unpaid sailors. As you read the story, ask yourself if you should be prayerfully seeking courage and boldness in your own witnessing challenges.

As I drove up to the gatehouse I could see signs of trouble. The police cruiser was there, its lights flashing. The gatehouse guards excitedly interpreting the crisis that had come to their otherwise quiet post. And in the midst, a group of dishevelled seamen—Filipino, Greek, Pakistani, Indian, Lebanese, and a few Egyptians. About fifteen in all. They had obviously left their ship in a hurry; some of them still had their work gloves on. They were evidently dressed for work, if you can call it dressed: broken boots, flimsy rain gear, and rags wrapped around their necks and faces to keep out the bitter cold. Their coveralls, or rather what remained of them, were hard with paint stains, rust and dirt. They looked overworked and underfed; some of them looked downright sick.

Their ship the m. v. *Borboros* had docked late the previous night after an almost five-week trip from the other side of the world. She had stopped in Montreal to get fitted out for entrance into the seaway and now, one day later, was ready to sail again. The m. v. *Borboros* was in a hurry. She was headed for Detroit to unload a very expensive cargo and was then due to load grain at the Lakehead for delivery to Cuba. All this had to happen before winter closed the St. Lawrence Seaway. There was no time to lose in Montreal.

But the captain and others in charge had forgotten one thing. The m. v. *Borboros* sailed by the grace of the people who had been hired to man her. And despite a full day in port after five solid weeks at sea, the crew was unhappy. The head office in Greece had forwarded no mail or wages to the ship's agents in Montreal, so crew members had no news of their families and no money to send home. Four men were visibly sick and had repeatedly asked to be sent to a medical facility—a request the captain refused. The ship could not run the risk of losing some men to a hospital ward before the precious cargo was delivered to Detroit.

To make things worse, the crew's living conditions were getting worse every day. Since the heating system in the crew's quarters had broken down, broken pipes, flooded cabins, and freezing temperatures were a daily reality for these men. They received no proper food or water, were provided with no facilities, and lived in rooms infested with rats and cockroaches. Some of the crew members had been on board for more than sixteen months.

For ships used to plowing tropical waters, coming to Montreal in the beginning of December and then going to the seaway is no picnic. A Lebanese or a Pakistani can hardly be expected to understand what he is signing when he puts his name to a document written in Greek and supported by "promises" and "assurances" of a master who is in need of a cheap crew. Furthermore, the ship is registered in Panama, the owners are in Greece, the charterers are in New York, the agents are in Montreal, and no one is really prepared to be bothered by hands that show signs of frostbite when those hands are from a Filipino seaman or an Indian deckhand.

The patience of an otherwise docile crew was coming to an end. One of their sick crew members, a sixty-one-year-old Pakistani man, was no longer able to face the continued strain on his exhausted body and "let go on his will to live." Slumped near one of the exits on board, he prepared to die from lack of medical attention, cold, frustration, exhaustion, and pure disgust.

That did it. As one man, the entire deck crew picked up their sick coworker, marched off the ship straight to the gatehouse, and there verbalized what not only the guard, but any untrained eye could see: human life was at stake.

We have a strange law in this place. The moment an unauthorized foreign seaman steps outside the gate enclosing the Federal Port Authority property, he is considered to be entering Canada illegally. By law these ravaged *Borboros* sailors could have been stripped of their dignity and hauled off to jail to await extradition. I had seen it happen before, and I didn't want to see it repeated with these people. I suggested they stay put in the guardhouse *inside* the gate while I saw their Pakistani friend to the medical clinic.

When I returned to the gatehouse, I arranged for a small delegation to accompany me on an inspection tour of the *Borboros*. I wanted to see for myself how bad conditions were.

As we slithered through half flooded, unimaginably dilapidated hallways, we entered the crew's messroom just in time to see a rat get himself caught in one of half a dozen rat traps set up around the room. The cabins were so infested by cockroaches that literally hundreds of them shot away in all directions as we opened the door.

Even as I climbed higher, to the officer's quarters and finally to the captain's cabin, I couldn't get away from the idea that I had entered some sort of dungeon. That's the strange thing about ships: some of them have the appearance of Hilton Hotel foyers while others look like blighted, condemned inner-city apartments. I had promised the crew that I would speak to the captain on their behalf in an effort to resolve at least some of their problems.

As the crookedness of the whole sordid situation came more and more into focus, I approached the captain with the prophet Malachi, an old hand (along with Habakkuk) in attacking corrupt situations.

To my own amazement, I found myself literally raving at this callous man who had kept his eyes closed to the dreadful condition his men were in (the people on whom, at sea, his very own safety depended). I informed him of the Lord's dealings with his people and of his relentless summons to those who are called by his name to at all times take up the plight of the stranger (the man who has no rights and therefore stands in need of our grace by exception). I set before him the stinging injunctions of Leviticus 19. I reminded him that he could not possibly expect this sort of thing to go unpunished and that, as a result, he was endangering his own soul.

To be quite frank, I had expected that at least during my speech (ah, well, you might as well call it a sermon, for after all, it really was a sermon) the captain would usher me to the door. But to my great amazement, after a short pause he simply said: "What do you suggest I should do?"

When I had recovered from my surprise at his reaction, I said: "Get an order out to pick up anyone in need of medical attention for appointment with the doctor. Make arrangements to get an extra supply of food (for Eastern people) on board. Have the ship fumigated. And summon money, every last cent to which your people are entitled. Let me muster twenty-seven winter coats out of the International Club for seafarers; you get the company to supply additional winter gear."

Most of my suggestions seemed impossible. In Montreal it was supper time, and the banks were closed. In Greece it was midnight, and everyone was asleep. A ten-thousand dollar fine hung over the company's heads if the delivery to Detroit was delayed even one day. And an expensive tugboat stood by, idling a costly engine at $500 per hour. So there was no way the captain could fill the crew's needs unless the *Borboros* stayed overnight and into the next day.

But the master gave in to the summons of the MASTER of us all. What did it, I still don't know. I'd like to think that it was the Spirit of God who firmly grabbed this man's soul and set him on a new course.

In fact, I have reasons to believe that that's just what happened. The ship *did* stay overnight. The money, along with twenty-seven coats, appeared the following day. The captain gave the crew an hour to go to the banks while rice and an assortment of other supplies were brought on board. A few hours later, when the m.v. *Borboros* left for the Great Lakes to deliver a cargo of "great" value, the men were warmer, happier, and healthier than they had been in months.

I wasn't sure if I'd ever see that crew again. But on Christmas Eve, there they were—the *Borboros* crew along with many other seafarers streaming into our small chapel to celebrate Christ's birth. We sang together—Roman Catholic Filipinos, Indian Hindus, Moslem Egyptians and Pakistani, Orthodox Greeks, and some who knew no God— and we listened together to the ever-thrilling news of God's concern for *all* people.

"His Master's Voice," by Hans Uittenbosch, *The Banner,* March 2, 1979, pp. 5–8

Thorn in the Flesh

Some of us have physical or emotional weaknesses that seem to make witnessing impossible: impaired hearing or eyesight, deafness, blindness, stuttering, mental blocks over people's names, physical deformities that make others withdraw, muscular dystrophy, a debilitating illness that saps every ounce of energy, and so forth.

What lessons can those who fear witnessing or even refuse to consider it because of obvious impairments learn from Paul's thorn in the flesh (2 Cor. 12:7–10)? We're not certain what Paul suffered from. He may have been afflicted with poor eyesight or stuttering or, as Paul Ramsey suggests, a malaria fever causing headaches "like a red-hot bar thrust through the forehead."

As you read this passage from Corinthians, look for at least three spiritual principles for dealing with a thorn in the flesh. Apply these guidelines to concrete cases among your personal acquaintances. Avoid being simplistic. Physical weaknesses can often be devastating in witness. After all, books and speeches on witnessing usually feature the beautiful extroverts who use superstar examples to impress audiences and readers. Try to come up with examples of thorn-in-the-flesh people who have made friendship witness work.

Fear as a Spiritual Problem

This chapter argues that everyone fears something and that our anxiety in witness is normal. Through practice, fear of the unknown begins to disappear.

However, fear of witnessing could be a spiritual problem also. Read 2 Corinthians 3:4–6 privately and spend a few minutes meditating on your own attitudes about witnessing. Could your reluctance need forgiveness and the Holy Spirit's renewal?

REFLECTIONS

Somebody Else's Job

Then I met Christians who had discovered a "theological" reason which enabled them not to bother about evangelism. They pointed out that in Ephesians 4:11 one of the gifts which ascended Christ had given to the Church was that of the evangelist. It was obvious that everyone was not an evangelist. If you were, you did the work. If you weren't, you didn't have to. It was as simple as that. To give them their due they did believe that the evangelists were to be encouraged and helped by us all, but only those who had the gift had to do the work. I decided that because I found evangelism so difficult, I obviously did not have the gift, and so all I had to do was pray for those who did. From then on, whenever I was reminded about the Great Commission to "go into all the world and preach the gospel," I immediately transferred it to the apostles to whom it was originally given and the evangelists whom Christ had provided. It had no direct application to me.

In spite of this I was still uneasy. I felt that I should be trying to lead people to Christ although now I didn't know why. But every time I tried, it was so hard that I concluded I did not have the gift.

Know and Tell The Gospel by John C. Chapman, pp. 10–11

God's Gospel

The gospel is God's gospel—he is its author and he states its content—and what a relief that is. We don't have to take the responsibility for the reactions of people to it. We didn't make it up! All we have to do is pass on a message. We will have to take full responsibility for the *way we tell* people the gospel but *not for the content of the gospel itself.* I heard about an undergraduate student who was so outraged by the gospel that he verbally attacked a Christian over the nature of the gospel. The Christian explained to the student that he must take that matter up with a much higher authority since it was not his gospel, but God's gospel. It is a challenge and a relief.

Know and Tell the Gospel by John C. Chapman, pp. 16–17

Our Comfort, Hope, and Peril

If there has been much disobedience perpetrated in the spirit of obedience, if there have been missions by the sword, by political power, by privileged position, by dollars, pounds, guilders, francs and Reichsmarks, if there have been, and if there are, missions based on the notion of white superiority, of western individualism, of the finality of western Christendom, all this God forgives and overcomes, and even uses, because there was in it all an element of obedience which He does not despise. It is not we who gather the Church, but He, through His word and Spirit. We may be bound by our limited vision, the Spirit is not bound. The perfect Means, availing Himself of our very imperfect means, will achieve the perfect End that lies very far beyond the horizon of the imperfect ends we envision. This is the comfort and the hope of the missionary community. But it is no less its peril. A doctrine that gives comfort in the awareness of the imperfection of our limited best may easily become a doctrine whereby we rationalize complacency, inertia and fruitlessness. But the price of complacency in God's kingdom is great. It is no small matter if on the one foundation that has been laid we build houses of wood, hay and stubble that shall be burned in the time of testing. It is no small matter if a grieved Spirit must achieve His ends without us, or in spite of us because we stood in His way and did not yield ourselves as supple instruments for His use.

Pentecost and Missions by Harry R. Boer, p. 208

Know Him

"I can't talk to anyone else about Christ because God just doesn't seem real to me."

This is a genuine obstacle. Sharing Jesus Christ is not basically talking about a moral code, our church, or Christian philosophy. It is introducing people to a person. And we can't introduce someone we ourselves have never met.

Timothy, Paul's young protégé, was apparently very timid. Paul shared with him the secret of his own confidence: "I am not ashamed, because *I know whom I have believed,* and am convinced that he is able to guard what I have entrusted to him for that day" (2 Tim. 1:7–8, 12, emphasis added).

Witnessing is taking a good look at Jesus and telling what we have seen. The better I know him, the less ashamed I am.

Good News Is for Sharing by Leighton Ford, p. 59

REFLECTIONS

Afraid of Offending?

Our problem in evangelism is not that we don't have enough information—it is that we don't know how to be ourselves. We forget we are called to be witnesses to what we have seen and know, not to what we don't know. The key is authenticity and obedience, not a doctorate in theology. We haven't grasped that it really is okay for us to be who we are, when we are with non-Christians, even if we don't have all the answers to their questions or if our knowledge of Scripture is limited.

But there is a deeper problem here. Our uneasiness with non-Christians reflects our uneasiness with our own humanity. Because we are not certain about what it means to be human (or spiritual, for that matter), we struggle in relating naturally, humanly, to the world. For example, many of us avoid evangelism for fear that we will offend someone. Yet how often have we told a non-Christian that that's why we are hesitating?

At the University of California, Berkeley campus, I met a coed one afternoon in Sproul Plaza. Our conversation moved to whether we believed in God. It was an easy, almost casual talk. I began telling her about Jesus and she seemed interested. But as I became more enthusiastic about what it meant to be a Christian, she seemed to withdraw emotionally. Still I kept on talking about Jesus— for want of knowing what else to do. But even though my mouth kept moving, I was very aware that I was turning her off. So there I was, having a private conversation with myself, trying to figure out how to stop, while I could hear myself talking to her about Christ.

Suddenly I realized how ridiculous all this was, so I said, "Look, I feel really bad. I *am* very excited about who God is and what he's done in my life. But I hate it when people push 'religion' on me. So if I'm coming on too strong will you just tell me?"

She looked at me in disbelief. "I can't believe you just said that. I mean, I cannot *believe* you honestly said that," she answered.

"Why?" I asked.

"Well, I never knew Christians were aware that we hate being recipients of a running monologue," she answered. (So much for my evangelistic skill.)

"Listen," I responded, "most Christians I know are very hesitant to share their faith *precisely* because they're afraid they'll offend."

"But as long as you let people know that you're aware of where they're coming from, you can say anything you want!" she responded immediately. "And you just tell Christians that I said so."

Out of the Salt Shaker by Rebecca M. Pippert, pp. 24–25

What If I Can't Answer a Question?

We all know this fear. There you are in the midst of a lively conversation about Christianity. Everything has worked out. You have expressed yourself well. Your friends are interested. The context is appropriate. You seem to be getting down to the real issues. And then *the question* is asked. It is a good question. It is a *real* question. In fact, it is a question you also would like an answer to. But that is the problem. You have no answer, nothing to say. So the whole conversation stumbles to an unsatisfying and embarrassing halt. As your friends drift away, the pit of your stomach tells you you've let your side down; you're a disappointment to Jesus.

The first thing that must be said in response to this fear is that it is largely hypothetical. Such a scenario generally happens only in our imaginations. True, people do have real questions about Christianity. But these are seldom totally new or completely unexpected questions. After years of work in university evangelism, Paul Little said that he could anticipate with 95 percent accuracy the questions that would be asked him in the course of an hour's conversation with non-Christians.

So, with a little work, we can learn how to respond to most questions—not in a trivial fashion, but thoughtfully because we have begun to think through the issues. There are many good books on this subject. For example, *Know Why You Believe* by Paul Little (InterVarsity Press) is an overview of the twelve most common questions students ask about Christianity. John Stott's book *Basic Christianity* (IVP) and John Warwick Montgomery's *History and Christianity* (Here's Life) provide valuable data about the historical foundations.

But what if after all this I get asked a question I cannot answer adequately? Simply admit your ignorance! Honesty is what counts in such situations, not total knowledge. No one expects you to have an encyclopedic knowledge of Christianity. However, after saying "I don't know," take the next step and offer to hunt for an answer. Answers do exist, and the process of searching them out will be as rewarding to you as to your friend. . . .

What offends people is not straight talk about faith, but the pretense of being a great guru with all the answers, which we spit out in rapid-fire, pious cliches laden with a sense of judgment and an aura of superiority. . . .

So the issue of witness is not how do I become good enough to share Christ. Rather it is how do I learn to be honest enough to share how Christ enables me to cope with my weakness. What intrigues non-Christians is the discovery of an imperfect person (as they are) with real problems (like theirs), coping with these in the awesome power of Christ.

Small Group Evangelism by Richard Peace, pp. 39–41, 44

REFLECTIONS

A Frightening Experience

Launching into a gospel presentation is an exciting, yet at the same time frightening, experience. I have personally gone through this transition hundreds of times, yet my pulse rate still accelerates when I realize that the moment is drawing near, and my mouth usually gets that "filled with cotton" feeling. Part of this is due to excitement and the resulting flow of adrenaline into your system. It is the Lord's way of preparing you so that your mind will be functioning at peak efficiency. But a large part of it is also due to fear, and it is this which can be most devastating. There are present in each one of us certain misgivings about entering into a situation where we, or our message, could be rejected. It is always frightening to venture into the unknown, especially when we are uncertain as to the nature of the reception that we will receive. Often these feelings of apprehension lead us to take the easy route of postponement or even complete cancellation. This is what must be guarded against.

Agape Evangelism—Roots that Reach Out by
Richard G. Korthals, p. 50

Don't Worry!

I used to worry constantly after witnessing to someone whether I did it right, if I should have said this or that, and so on. The Scripture calls us to excellence, but it also says the Spirit will give us what we need for tough situations (Mark 13:11). To be anxious about whether we have witnessed in exactly the "right way" implies there is some outside perfect standard that we are being judged by. But there is no magic formula; there is no absolute and correct way to witness every time. We are called to do the very best we can, and then trust the Holy Spirit to speak to a person through what we say and do.

Out of the Saltshaker by Rebecca M. Pippert, p. 129

The Hardest Part

The hardest part in evangelism is starting. We'll do anything except begin. We do another training course; we read another book. We form yet another committee and go to prayer meetings about it. But if you've not started—it's time. The best way to learn is to do it. None of us is much good at the beginning.

Know and Tell the Gospel by John C. Chapman, p. 113

REFLECTIONS

Will We Succeed?

Jesus Christ gives us the promise that meets our most basic need. "Surely I will be with you always," he says, "to the very end of the age."

Roland Allen, a famous missionary thinker, explained that "the promised presence of Christ is not a reward offered those who obey, but rather the assurance that those commanded will be able to obey." One of the most common misunderstandings of evangelism is that it's something *we do* for Jesus Christ. But if I understand what Jesus is saying to us here, he is telling us that evangelism is something he does through us. It's not that Jesus Christ is saying, "Hey, you go out into the world there and do something for me." He is saying, "As you go through your life, through the struggles, the pains, the joys—to school, to work, to play, I am with you and I am working through you. I am making my authority known in all the earth. You trust me. You obey me, and I will be with you, and you will see that it is going to happen.

It is tremendously important to get this into our hearts. Sharing the good news is *God's* mission. Evangelism is his work. At the very beginning of his ministry Jesus said, "The Spirit of the Lord is upon me." There you have the Trinity: the Lord (Father), the Spirit, and the Son. God is working out his plan in the world, sovereignly working all things according to his purpose. His purpose is to establish his Kingdom, to build his Body the Church, to make disciples. In order to carry this out, all authority has been given to Jesus Christ. The Holy Spirit is the one who empowers the Body of Christ. The Holy Spirit is the one through whom Jesus Christ carries out his work and the Father's purpose through the Church. Evangelism is not just a *commission* that God gives to us. It is *co-mission*.

When we share our faith, we are actually working in partnership with the triune God.

Understanding this frees me from many of my hang-ups and problems. It frees me from laziness and unconcern. How can I sit back and not care, when the living God, the Creator himself, is actually calling me to be a partner with him in the greatest work in the world! It frees me from pride, the haughty arrogance that turns more people away from Christ than it draws to him. It saves me from the fear of failure and despair. I don't let the fear of failure keep me from sharing my faith, nor do I let it lead me to manipulate people in a dishonest way so that I can get "results." I can be concerned for results, but I can leave people in God's hands, because this is his work, and he is doing it with me and through me. As writer/lecturer Ann Kiemel says, "God and love and I are out to change the world. I may be just an ordinary, everyday young woman, but in little ways everyday I am going to make a difference. You wait, you'll see."

This is the kind of evangelism to which Jesus Christ is calling you and me.

Jesus—Aslan—the mighty Christ, the moving Christ, the mysterious Christ is saying, "Get on my back—let's go for a ride—let's make some new Aslan people. Just hang on, and let's get going!"

Good News Is for Sharing by Leighton Ford, p. 59

116

BIBLIOGRAPHY

ALDRICH, EIMS AND HENDRICKS. *Lifestyle Evangelism and Follow-up: A Navigator Video Seminar for the Church.* Colorado Springs, CO: NavPress, 1983. Copyright © 1983 by The Navigators. Used by permission of NavPress, Colorado Springs, CO. All rights reserved. For copies call 1-800-366-7788.

ALDRICH, JOSEPH C. *Life-Style Evangelism.* Portland, OR: Multnomah Press, 1985. Copyright © 1985 by Multnomah Press. Used by permission of Multnomah Press, Portland, OR 97266.

BAYLY, JOSEPH. *The Gospel Blimp.* Havertown, PA: Windward Press, 1960. Copyright © 1960, Joseph Bayly. Used by permission of David C. Cook Publishing Co., Elgin, IL.

BOER, HARRY R. *Pentecost and Missions.* Grand Rapids, MI: Wm. B. Eerdmans Publishing Co., 1961. Used by permission of Wm. B. Eerdmans Publishing Co.

CHAPMAN, JOHN C. *Know and Tell the Gospel.* Colorado Springs, CO: NavPress, 1985. Copyright © 1985 by The Navigators. Used by permission of NavPress, Colorado Springs, CO. All rights reserved. For copies call 1-800-366-7788.

CLINE, WILLIAM C. *Growing as a Caring Community.* Valley Forge, PA: American Baptist Churches, 1979. Used by permission of the author.

COOPER, DALE. "Proud to Bear My Father's Name," *The Banner.* June 16, 1986. Copyright © 1986, CRC Publications, a Ministry of the Christian Reformed Church. Reprinted with permission.

EARECKSON, JONI and ESTES, STEVE. *A Step Further.* Grand Rapids, MI: Zondervan Publishing House, 1978. Copyright © 1978 by Joni Eareckson and Steve Estes. Used by permission of Zondervan Publishing House.

EPPINGA, JACOB D. *Of Cabbages and Kings.* Grand Rapids, MI: Zondervan Publishing House, 1974. Used by permission of the author.

FORD, LEIGHTON. *The Christian Persuader.* New York, Harper and Row, 1966.

FORD, LEIGHTON. *Good News Is for Sharing.* Elgin, IL: David C. Cook Publishing Co., 1977. Copyright © 1977 by David C. Cook Publishing Co. Used by permission.

FOWLER, JAMES W. *Stages of Faith.* San Francisco, CA: Harper and Row, 1981.

FRANKL, VIKTOR, E. *Man's Search for Meaning.* Boston, MA: Beacon Press, 1959. Used by permission of Beacon Press.

GREEN, MICHAEL. *Evangelism in the Early Church.* Grand Rapids, MI: Wm. B. Eerdmans Publishing Co., 1970. Copyright © 1970, Michael Green. Used in North America by permission of Wm. B. Eerdmans Publishing Co.

GRIFFIN, JOHN HOWARD. *Black Like Me.* Boston, MA: Signet Books, 1960. Copyright © 1960, 1961, 1977 by John Howard Griffin. Used by permission of Houghton Mifflin Company, Boston.

KORTHALS, RICHARD G. *Agape Evangelism— Roots that Reach Out.* Wheaton, IL: Tyndale Publishing, 1980. Used by permission of the author.

KUIPER, R. B. *God-Centered Evangelism*. Grand Rapids, MI: Baker Book House, 1961. Used by permission of Baker Book House.

LEWIS, C. S. *Mere Christianity*. New York: Macmillan Publishing Co., Inc., 1952. Copyright © 1943, 1945, 1952 Macmillan Publishing Co., Inc. Used by permission of William Collins Sons & Co., Ltd., London.

LEWIS, C. S. *The Voyage of the Dawn Treader*. New York: Macmillan Publishing Co., Inc., 1952. Copyright © 1952 Macmillan Publishing Co., Inc. Used by permission of William Collins Sons & Co., Ltd., London.

LITTLE, PAUL. *How to Give Away Your Faith*. Downers Grove, IL: InterVarsity Press, 1966. Copyright © 1966, revised edition © 1988 by Marie Little. Used by permission of InterVaristy Press, P. O. Box 1400, Downers Grove, IL 60515.

McGINNIS, ALAN LOY. *The Friendship Factor*. Minneapolis, MN: Augsburg Publishing House, 1979.

PEACE, RICHARD. *Small Group Evangelism*. Downers Grove, IL: InterVarsity Press, 1985. Copyright © 1985 by InterVarsity Christian Fellowship of the USA. Used by permission of InterVarsity Press, P. O. Box 1400, Downers Grove, IL 60515.

PETERSEN, JIM. *Evangelism as a Lifestyle*. Colorado Springs, CO: NavPress, 1980. Copyright © 1980 by The Navigators. Used by permission of NavPress, Colorado Springs, CO. All rights reserved. For copies call 1-800-366-7788.

PIPPERT, REBECCA MANLEY. *Out of the Saltshaker and into the World*. Downers Grove, IL: InterVarsity Press, 1979. Copyright © 1979 by InterVarsity Christian Fellowship of the USA. Used by permission of InterVarsity Press, P. O. Box 1400, Downers Grove, IL 60515.

PRIOR, KENNETH F.W. *The Gospel in Pagan Society*. Downers Grove, IL: InterVarsity Press, 1975. Copyright © 1975 by Kenneth F.W. Prior.

SCHAAP, JAMES C. "My Mother's Tears," *The Banner*. September 15, 1986. Copyright 1986, CRC Publications, a Ministry of the Christian Reformed Church. Reprinted with permission.

SMEDES, LEWIS. *Forgive and Forget: Healing the Hurts We Don't Deserve*. New York: Harper and Row, Publishers, Inc., 1984. Copyright © 1984 by Lewis Smedes. Used by permission of Harper & Row, Publishers, Inc.

SMEDES, LEWIS. *Love Within Limits*. Grand Rapids, MI: Wm. B. Eerdmans Publishing Co., 1978.

UITTENBOSCH, HANS. "His Master's Voice," *The Banner*. March 2, 1979. Copyright © 1979, CRC Publications, a Ministry of the Christian Reformed Church. Reprinted with permission.

WATSON, DAVID. *I Believe in Evangelism*. Grand Rapids, MI: Wm. B. Eerdmans Publishing Co., 1977. Used by permission of Wm. B. Eerdmans Publishing Co.

WHITE, JOHN. "Metamorphosis," *HIS Magazine*, December, 1963. Used by permission of *U Magazine* (formerly *HIS Magazine*), a publication of InterVarsity Press.